KEYS TO CALMING THE FUSSY BABY

William Sears, M.D.

Pediatrician
Assistant Clinical Professor of
Pediatrics at the University of
Southern California

BARRON'S

New York • London • Toronto • Sydney

Cover photo by Scott Barrow, Inc., Cold Spring, NY

All inquiries should be addressed to:
Barron's Educational Series, Inc.
250 Wireless Boulevard
Hauppauge, New York 11788

Library of Congress Catalog Card No. 90-25343

International Standard Book No. 0-8120-4538-6

Library of Congress Cataloging in Publication Data
Sears, William, M.D.
    Keys to calming the fussy baby / William Sears.
        p.   cm.—(Barron's parenting keys)
    ISBN 0-8120-4538-6
    1. Infants—Care.   2. Crying in infants   3. Infants—Sleep.
    I. Title.   II. Series.
HQ774.S44   1991
305.23′2—dc20   90-25343
                                                                        CIP

PRINTED IN THE UNITED STATES OF AMERICA
1234   5500   98765432

CONTENTS

CONTENTS

INTRODUCTION

You cannot make a baby go to sleep. You can, however, create a sleep-inducing environment that encourages sleep to overtake him. Instead of simply "letting him cry it out," the following keys will help you to help your baby sleep better and stay asleep longer. The approach I take to nighttime parenting has one goal in mind—to help your baby grow up with the attitude that sleep is not a state to be feared but a pleasant state to enter into.

Having a restless baby can bring out the best and the worst in a parent. The approach I take in this book is designed to help you and your baby bring out the best in each other. Fussy and sleepless babies—I prefer to call them high-need babies—are born that way. You do not cause them to fuss and awaken. They do it because of their own temperaments, not because of your parenting abilities. Babies have a wide range of temperaments. Some settle easily and sleep well; others have more difficulty adjusting to life outside the womb and need creative comforting and sleep-inducing techniques to help them calm and settle.

In the following keys we will present the tools to help your baby fuss less and sleep better. My goal in this book is to help *everyone* in the family enjoy a good night's sleep.

1

1

~~~~~~

PROFILE OF THE FUSSY BABY

O ur first three babies were relatively easy. As a pediatrician I really did not understand why many parents become so troubled about their baby's fussiness. Then our fourth baby, Hayden, turned our relatively peaceful home upside down. Hayden came wired differently. When it came to sleeping and eating, the term "schedule" had no meaning to her. Whenever we put her down she cried. We played pass the baby: Hayden would spend hours in my wife's arms, and when Martha gave out, I would carry her. Sometimes we would call in the reserves of friends and relatives to hold Hayden. We could not leave her or she would fuss. Everywhere Bill and Martha went Hayden was sure to go. She slept irregularly during the day and at night. She was inconsistently consoled; what worked one day did not work the next, and very early on Hayden merited the label "demanding." There were days when we were sympathetic, and there were days when we were exhausted, and there were days we were downright angry. If she had been our first baby we would constantly have wondered what we were doing wrong, but we started life the same way we had with our other babies. It was then that we realized that fussy babies are seldom made; they come that way. Babies fuss because of their own temperament, not because of our parenting abilities.

The fussy baby, alias the high-need baby. The term "fussy baby" is unfair. It implies that either the baby is failing, the parents are failing, or the whole relationship is failing. It is an unjustly negative term. During years of parenting a fussy baby and counseling thousands of parents of similar babies, one statement has always come out: "She has such high needs." Why not call these "high-need babies"? It is a kinder term, and more accurately describes why these babies act the way they do and what level of parenting they need. It is a positive and uplifting term, sounding intelligent and special. Isn't that what all parents like to hear?

As soon as I mention the term "high-need baby" I notice an immediate relief on the part of parents. By the time they come to me they have been bombarded with conflicting advice: "You carry her too much," "You don't carry her enough," "You're spoiling her; why can't you stop her cries?" The basic message of all this advice is "It's your fault that your baby fusses." The term "high-need baby" relieves the guilt from the parents and places these special babies in the category they deserve. If you are in the profession of offering advice to young parents or if you have a friend with a fussy baby, use the term "high-need baby" and you will start your relationship off on a much more positive note.

Twelve years later, Hayden is a wonderfully creative, deeply sensitive and delightfully exuberant person to be around. Over the years she has brought out the best and the worst in us. Her needs have not lessened; they have only changed. She is now a high-need teenager. And we have survived.

I have pulled from my gallery the most common characteristics parents have shared with me about their high-need babies. They may not have all of these characteristics all the time, but all have some of these characteristics some of the time.

3

Supersensitive. These babies have a short fuse; they are easily bothered; they startle easily and settle poorly. This sensitivity causes them to adjust slowly to unfamiliar environments and caregivers and often to have a high degree of anxiety around strangers. Even the slightest change in their environment can set them off. Initially parents may find this supersensitivity exhausting, but with proper understanding and guidance, this early liability can be turned into an asset later. These babies often become very warm and caring children who are sympathetic to the needs of their peers.

Intense. These babies put a lot of energy into their behavior. They cry loudly, laugh with gusto, and are quick to protest if their "meals" are not served instantly. One tired father said, "She's in high gear all the time." High-need babies seem to feel things more deeply and react more forcefully. They are capable of forming deep and lasting attachments. They do not become shallow individuals. Because they demand and need strong attachments to their parents, their subsequent attachments are also strong, and they grow up with one of the most beautiful of adult characteristics—the capability of developing intimacy.

"I just can't put him down." Parents-to-be often have unrealistic expectations of a baby lying contentedly in a crib, gazing at dangling mobiles and only needing to be picked up at dutiful intervals for feeding and changing. This is not typical of a high-need baby or of most babies. They do not have the ability to soothe themselves; their caregivers must soothe them. Parents often say, "He just can't relax." Mother's lap is his chair, father's arms and chest his crib, and mother's breast his pacifier. These babies are quick to reject mother substitutes such a cuddlies, soothers and pacifiers. They demand a higher standard of soothing. High-need babies are "up" babies, not "down" babies—they are "up" in arms most of the time.

4

"**Hyperactive, hypertonic.**" These babies arch their backs and frequently attempt to do back dives during nursing or while being held. Fathers have reported, "His motor is stuck in fast idle." One photographer father said to me, "I can't take a still shot of my baby."

"**Draining.**" Parents relate, "He wears me out." Parents of high-need babies are inevitably tired.

"**Wants to nurse all the time.**" If the baby had a vocabulary, the term "schedule" wouldn't be in it. They need long periods of extra-nutritive sucking for comfort. They often "marathon" nurse every two to three hours. Not only do they have a greater need to nurse, they nurse longer. They are notoriously slow to wean; it is not unusual for a high-need baby to nurse well into the second or third year.

"**Unpredictable, unsatisfied.**" These babies are inconsistently appeased. What works one day may not work the next. As one exhausted mother exclaimed, "Just as I feel I have the game won, he just keeps upping the ante!"

"**Awakens frequently.**" "Why does she need more of everything but sleep?" lamented a tired mother. These super-aware babies do not settle easily. They seldom need naps, but certainly their parents do. The "brightness" that these babies often reveal as older children is reflected in their night-waking behavior—as if they have an internal light bulb that cannot turn off.

"**Uncuddly.**" This is the most difficult of "high-need" babies. While most babies will melt easily into the arms and over the shoulders of their caregivers, the high-need baby will often stiffen his arms and legs, protesting against intimate physical contact. While most high-need babies crave physical contact and love being swaddled, the uncuddly babies are much slower to nestle in parents' arms. They need a special type of cuddling that we will discuss later.

"Demanding." This is the most usual character trait of high-need babies. Mothers often say, "I just can't get to him fast enough." The babies' signals convey a real sense of urgency. "Red alerts" dominate their crying vocabulary. They have no respect for delayed gratification and do not readily accept alternatives. Wishing a breast and offered a bottle, they protest vehemently. Being demanding is necessary in order to receive the higher level of parenting that will enable them to reach their fullest potential.

The high-need baby—a blessing or a trial? Early on, the high-need baby is uncuddly, unsatisfied. There are a lot of negative feelings as parents adjust to life with this type of baby. Eventually parents begin to see their babies in a different light and use such positive descriptions as "interesting," "challenging," "bright," "rewarding."

2

~~~~~~

UNDERSTANDING YOUR BABY'S TEMPERAMENT

Most parents-to-be ask, "What is our baby going to be like?" while they're waiting out those nine long months. It won't be long before you will have a clue about your baby's temperament. "Temperament" is how your baby behaves, how she acts, the intent within her that makes her act the way she does. Your baby will probably receive certain labels such as "easy," "difficult," "mellow," "fussy," or "demanding." With time, the child's reaction to the environment and its influence upon her develop this inner temperament into personality—meaning the outward expression of the child's inner temperament. Perhaps the child you had hoped for is not the one you got! I will now discuss what contributes to baby's temperament and why she acts the way she does, and offer practical suggestions on adjusting to the less-than-perfect baby.

Nature versus nurture. For decades, psychologists have debated the nature-versus-nurture question: is it primarily heredity or environment that determines a child's temperament? Today most scientists agree that a child's temperament is not a blank slate onto which caregivers can write a set of rules that will cause the child to act the way the caregivers wish. Neither is a child's temperament permanently cast in cement. Temperament is due to both *nature* (genetic influence) and *nurture* (the parenting style of the caregiving environment). Over the past 30 years, child development researchers have been increasingly aware of how the quality and quantity of mothering and fathering can affect a child's development. The "goodness of fit" principle describes one of the most powerful influences on a baby's temperament. This principle states that how a baby fits into her caregiving environment will positively or negatively affect the development of her personality.

While in the womb, the fetus fits perfectly into her environment. There will never be another environment in which the baby fits so harmoniously, an environment in which baby's needs are automaticallly and predictably met. The womb environment is very well organized physically and emotionally. Birth suddenly disrupts this organization. During the months following birth, the baby tries to retain a sense of organization. Birth and adaptation of postnatal life bring out the temperament of a baby, since for the first time she must do something to have her needs met. She is forced to act, to "behave." She must make an effort to get the things she needs in her caregiving environment. If hungry, she cries. If her needs are simple and she can get what she needs easily, she is labeled an "easy baby"; she fits. If a baby does not adapt readily to what is expected of her, she is labeled a difficult baby. She doesn't easily fit. Some babies fit easily into their environment, some do not. To understand the principle of fit, I have developed the *need level concept.*

The need level concept. Every baby comes wired with a certain temperament for a reason. Every baby possesses a certain level of need that must be fulfilled if she is to develop to her maximum potential. It stands to reason that an infant would also come wired with a temperament to be able to communicate these needs. The early language cues of a baby are a language of need. They are referred to as attachment-promoting behaviors, the most noteworthy of which is the infant's cry. An infant with a high level of needs also comes programmed with an intense way of communicating these needs. For example, babies who need a lot of holding in order to thrive will protest if they are put down.

Some babies are labeled easy babies. They are content in a variety of caregiving circumstances. They don't cry much because their needs are easily met. They are somewhat consistent and predictable in their needs and adapt easily to a variety of schedules and parenting styles. (These are the babies everyone else has!) High-need babies, on the other hand, may be supersensitive to changes in their environment. I wish parents would view the demanding quality of such babies as a positive character trait that has survival benefits for the baby. If the baby were endowed with high needs yet lacked the ability to communicate these needs, her survival would be threatened. This baby would not develop to her full potential.

The most common example of demanding behavior in a high-need baby is the infant who cries whenever she is put down. Before birth, baby has a sense of oneness with the mother. After birth, the mother knows that the baby is now a separate person, but the baby does not feel separate. The baby still has a sense of oneness with mother. Birth has changed only the manner in which this oneness is expressed. This baby will protest or fuss if her attachment to the mother is disrupted. She needs to continue the attachment a bit longer. Fortunately she has the ability to demand this, and if the baby's needs are heard and fulfilled, she fits. She is in harmony with her environment. She feels right.

What happens if a baby's needs remain unfulfilled because her demands have gone unheard? A need that is not fulfilled never completely goes away, but results in inner stress that sooner or later manifests itself as undesirable behavior—such as anger, aggression, withdrawal, or rejection. This baby does not feel right and therefore does not act right. A baby who does not act right is less of a joy to parent, and baby and parents drift farther and farther apart. The parent become less adept at caregiving and the baby becomes less motivated to signal her needs. The entire parent-child relationship operates at a low level.

The need level concept leads us to a very important point I wish new parents to fully understand: *Your baby fusses primarily because of her own temperament and not because of your parenting abilities.* Babies fuss because they have to in order to fit. However, the responsiveness of the caregiving environment does play a part in determining whether or not the baby's demanding temperament is channeled into desirable or undesirable personality traits.

Temperament combinations. The temperament of the baby greatly affects the caregiving behavior of the parents. I learned this one day when a mother confided to me, "Our baby absolutely brings out the best and the worst in me." Current research shows that the infant is an active participant in shaping the parents' behavior so that they can both fit into a style of parenting that brings out the best in each other.

There are two variables that lead to a good match or fit between mother and baby: the attachment-promoting or communicating skills of the baby and the responsiveness or sensitivity of the mother. Here are five of the most common examples of temperament matching and their outcome:

1. *An easy baby with a responsive mother.* This is a combination that will result in a good fit. Because mothers tend to feel that the "goodness" of their babies reflects their effectiveness as

mothers, the mother in this case is likely to be delighted with the fit. Because easy babies are less demanding, they do not always initiate interactions with their caregivers. But a responsive mother makes up for this by taking great care to initiate responses from her baby.

2. *An easy baby with a more restrained mother.* This may not be as good a fit. Because the easy baby is not very demanding, a less responsive mother may extend relatively little effort in developing her mothering skills. She may feel that the baby doesn't seem to need her much and then seek more challenging activities elsewhere. In this match, not only does the mother fail to bring out the best in the baby, but the baby does not bring out the best in the mother.

3. *A high-need baby with good attachment-promoting behaviors coupled with a responsive mother.* This is usually the best fit. Each is likely to bring out the best in the other. The baby has high needs and has a corresponding temperament to communicate these needs. Mother, because she is open and responsive to the baby, develops a higher level of mothering skills to meet the needs of her baby. Even when the mother is confused at not being able to easily identify her baby's needs, she experiments with different responses until she finds one that works. Mother learns to nurture better and baby learns to communicate better, and the entire mother-infant relationship operates at a higher level. Because this baby receives the consistent and predictable nurturing response that she needs, the baby learns to trust and she refines

11

her ability to communicate her needs. This makes it easier for mother to identify baby's needs and to comfort her. Baby and mother become mutually sensitive to each other. Because mother is able to listen better, baby learns to cry better, and the pair continually work to bring out the best in one another.

4. *A high-need baby with poor attachment-promoting skills and a responsive mother.* These babies, often known as "noncuddlers," are slow to warm up to caregiving. They appear not to need a lot of nurturing, but in reality they do. These babies may appear to be easy babies, but in reality they are high-need babies in easy-baby disguise. Parenting these babies may be difficult initially because parents do not receive the feedback of appreciation they would get from a more cuddly baby who obviously enjoys being held and cared for. With a responsive mother, this type of baby usually does well. The mother does her best to initiate interaction and help the baby develop better attachment-promoting skills. These babies need the best response a parent can give in order for the best in themselves to develop.

5. *A high-need baby and a restrained caregiver.* This pair is at highest risk for not developing a good fit. Neither one brings out the best in each other because the baby's language and needs are not understood. In this situation the baby may be endowed with good attachment-promoting skills, but because the mother does not develop her nurturing skills the baby has not refined his need-communicating skills.

Many well-meaning parents are particularly vulnerable to this temperament mismatch, because of an unfortunate preconception that new parents should not listen to their baby out of fear of being manipulated. Grandparents or friends may lead vulnerable new parents to feel that they are being poor disciplinarians if they give consistent nurturant responses to their baby. This quickly becomes a no-win situation. The parents lose their chance to develop intuitive nurturing skills because of their fear of listening and responding to their baby. The baby loses the opportunity to develop better communication skills and refine some rough edges in her temperament.

This is why throughout this book I have two goals in helping parents survive and thrive with their restless baby: 1) improving the sensitivity of the parents, and 2) organizing the temperament of the baby.

3

‸‸

UNDERSTANDING YOUR BABY'S CRIES

The infant's cry is designed for her own survival and her parents' development. It is a two-way communication network in which the infant is programmed to give a signal and the parents—the receivers—are uniquely programmed to respond. Let's examine both parts of this communication network. In the first few months of life, a baby's needs are greatest at a time when his skills to communicate these needs are least. A baby cannot tell us what he needs. To fill the gap in time until the baby is able to "speak our language," he has been given a language called a cry, and this is how it works. The baby senses a need. The realization of this need reflexively triggers the sudden inspiration of air, followed by a forceful expiration. The forcefully expired air passes through the vocal cords, and the vibrating cords produce a sound we call a cry.

A cry is not just a sound; it is a signal. Cries are triggered by need, and babies will use different signals for different needs. The stronger the need-stimulus, the more forcibly the baby expels air, and the vocal cords vibrate more rapidly. This accounts for the difference in the quality of the sounds produced. Researchers call these unique sounds *cry prints*, which are as unique to each baby as fingerprints. One day I was discussing the characteristics of the infant's cry with an engineer friend whose specialty is developing alert signals. He concluded that the infant's cry meets the four qualities of a perfect signal. First, the cries of early infancy are of reflex origin; they are *automatic.* They flow naturally in reponse to a need. The tiny infant does not have to stop and think, "Now what kind of cry will get me fed?" As these initial reflexes are responded to, they are later refined into more purposeful and deliberate crying, and then, as the infant learns to trust his communicating ability (and your responding ability), the crying is even better refined into true language. In essence, the baby eventually learns to "cry better."

Second, the signal is *easily generated;* the baby initiates crying with very little effort. Third, this signal is *disturbing* enough to alert the caregiver to attend to the baby and stop the cry, but not so disturbing as to promote an avoidance response. Fourth, the cry *vanishes* when the need for it has passed. These features make the infant's cry a perfect signal to ensure the survival of the baby and the sensitivity development of the parents. What is even more fascinating about your infant's cry is the effect it has on the parents, especially the mother. Studies have shown that mothers are designed to give a nurturant response to their baby's cry, not to restrain themselves. If you were to examine a mother-baby pair in a laboratory and attach the mother to various devices that measure the effect of her baby's cry on her physiology, the following interesting changes occur. In response to her baby's cry the blood flow to a mother's breast doubles, the mothering hormones increase and she has a biological urge to respond to her baby's cry. So you see, even scientific studies fail to validate the time-honored "Let your baby cry it out" advice.

Let's examine the cry of a typical baby to understand how different parts of the cry have different meanings. The opening seconds of a baby's cry have a very special quality called an attachment-promoting sound, meaning it is designed to trigger the desire in the listener to give a nurturant response

15

to the cry. It promotes attachment between mother and baby. If mother responds immediately to the opening sounds of her baby's cries, the baby's cry stops, or at least lessens. Mother feels right because she has followed her biological instinct and in so doing has increased her sensitivity. The baby, because his cries were immediately listened to, has learned to stop crying. The sensitivity of the mother and the trust level of the baby become better developed.

4

SHOULD BABY CRY IT OUT?

Every day in the world of tired parents and night-waking babies, exhausted and vulnerable mothers are given the canned recipe for getting their babies to sleep through the night: "Put her in her room, shut the door, put cotton in your ears and let her cry. She will cry two hours the first night, one hour the second night, and so on and so on and in a week she will be sleeping through the night." Recent baby books offer numerous methods of keeping babies asleep, all based on letting them cry it out. It's easy for someone else to advise you to let your baby cry it out; he is not the one who has to listen to the 3:00 A.M. wailing. The "cry it out" adviser also has no biological attachment to the baby, and therefore is not bothered when baby cries.

Most mothers whom I have interviewed on the subject of letting their baby cry it out have responded, "I just can't do it." Here's why you can't do it. The cry of an infant is more than just a sound. It is a signal intended to influence the behavior of another. The signal of the infant's cry releases the mother's emotions. It does something to the mother, and that is what makes this mother-baby crying communication network so special. In response to her own baby's cry, the mother's body chemistry changes. When a mother hears or sees her own baby cry, she experiences a surge of hormones within her body and an increase in blood flow to her breasts that triggers the urge to pick up and nurse the baby. There

17

are two parts to this communication network—the transmitter (the baby) and the receiver (the parent). The value of the cry depends upon the infant properly emitting it and the listener's correctly perceiving it. When the baby's nighttime cries are properly attended to, he learns to trust that his actions can affect others. The infant learns that he has value. This is the beginning of self-esteem. A mother who follows her instinctive urge to respond properly to her crying baby develops her own sensitivity. The more she responds to her baby's cry the more sensitive she becomes to the meaning of the baby's language. The combination of baby's trust and mother's sensitivity gets nighttime parenting off to the right start.

Building up a sensitivity to your baby's cues is one way your intuition matures. Promptly responding to your baby's cry helps to develop your sensitivity. Restraining yourself from responding makes you insensitive, and insensitivity gets a new mother in trouble. Guilt is a healthy reaction when some inner set of rules connected with some inner instinct has not been followed. This is exactly what happened in the mother who described herself as feeling guilty. She allowed herself to do something that went against her inner mothering rules, and naturally she did not feel right about it. Most of the mother's guilt feelings are caused by outside advice that runs contrary to her own intuition. The advisors are the ones who should be bothered by guilt, not the mother.

Another reason I have concerns about the wisdom of the crying-it-out approach is that it is often the lazy approach. Advising a mother to restrain her intuitive response to her crying baby at night presumes that the baby is crying not out of a basic need to be held and comforted, but out of a wish to annoy the parents or keep the parents awake. Parents who are too quick to jump on the restraining type of approach to getting their baby to sleep often fail to create more humane nighttime parenting methods. Parents who have bucked the experts and followed their intuition eventually develop more sensitive and creative sleep-inducing techniques in which they all sleep better and they feel right about their methods.

The cry-it-out approach also supposes that there are no medical reasons for the baby waking up at night. I have seen medical reasons for night waking overlooked because it was immediately assumed that the baby was spoiled, was manipulating parents and simply needed to cry it out.

Does letting the baby cry work? When I interview parents who allow themselves to be talked into letting their babies cry it out in the middle of the night, they often tell me it doesn't work. An occasional parent will report that the baby, when left to cry, did stop waking up, but the effects were less than desirable. Laurie, an exhausted mother of a night-waking baby, in desperation succumbed to the restraint response advice. "I plugged my ears and let him cry," she said. "But the baby's cries got louder and finally I couldn't stand it any longer and went in to him. Boy, was he mad! I'll never do that again."

Another failure of the restrained response approach was shared with me by a mother whose doctor advised her to let her night-waking baby cry it out. "I couldn't stand it any longer, and finally I went to nurse him back to sleep. We both sat there in the rocking chair crying together. It took me twice as long to nurse him back to sleep as if I had gone to him immediately. The next day he was clinging to me all day long." This mother learned an important fact of midnight mothering: the more quickly a cry is responded to, the easier it is to turn it off. The baby's clinginess the next day was an emotional response to his trust having been temporarily shattered. The defense of the unresponsive approach is that a baby must learn to sleep. These advisors claim that if one always intervenes to help the baby get back to sleep, the baby will never become a self-soother and will never be able to put himself back to sleep. There is some truth to this teaching. Babies who are used to having a parent nurse or rock them back to sleep do learn to rely on the parent for help. Which is better to rely on—a trusted parent or a synthetic bear? a raggedy blanket or a callused thumb? By not responding to baby's cries, you are not really teaching the baby to sleep; you are teaching your baby that cries have no communicative value. When cries are not responded to, the baby may fall back to sleep on his own, but this is a sign of withdrawal following the disappointment of not being listened to. By not giving in to your baby you are teaching him to give up. I have great difficulty with the wisdom of this approach. It is night training, it is not nighttime parenting. We train pets, we *parent* children.

"But you are creating a habit" is another way to justify the restraint approach. There is often a very fine line between a habit and a need. A habit is usually considered to be a pattern of behavior acquired by frequent repetition that a person can get of rid of with no resulting harm. A need, on the other hand, is necessary for the proper functioning of the individual. A habit, if not responded to, will easily go away. A need does not go away so easily. An unfulfilled need is never completely erased; it is only temporarily suppressed and will flare up again in a different way. In general, if you recognize that your child's desire for nighttime parenting is a need to be met and not a habit to be broken, you both will eventually receive a payoff of fewer sleepless nights once the child's need is fulfilled.

The baby's temperament also influences whether or not the "let your baby cry" advice should be used. High-need babies rarely respond to the restraint approach. They learn to cry harder, longer, and with more disturbing cries. These babies send the unmistakable message that they need a high level of nighttime parenting. These babies are also endowed with a temperament that stimulates them to protest vehemently if their needs are not met.

Babies with easier temperaments usually do not exhibit night-waking cries that activate the red-alert response in the mother. Easy babies seem more capable of self-soothing and may not elicit as prompt a response to their night-waking cries. Be especially vigilant about the so-called "easy baby." These babies are a mixed blessing. They are endowed with self-soothing abilities, which take some pressure off the mother. However, they also lack certain attachment-promoting behaviors (for example, protest cries when a need is not being filled) that develop their personalities and their mothers' skills.

Experienced mothers can often tell a "red alert" cry from a "hold off a bit" cry by the demanding nature of the cry and how quickly it diminishes. The cries of a high-need baby usually build up momentum until anyone in earshot must respond. The cries of an easy baby may diminish more quickly, and the baby may resettle without a parent's help. Whether or not to respond to a baby's night-waking cries is a judgment call. *Only the mother has the sensitivity to make this judgment.*

5

TEACHING YOUR BABY TO CRY BETTER

Some high-need babies have a particularly disturbing quality of cry which, as parents say, "drives me bananas." Here is an example of how you can begin mellowing your baby's cries in the newborn period. A recent patient of mine, Jeffrey, minutes after birth began a shrill, ear-piercing cry that almost cleared the delivery room. He did not have an attachment-promoting cry, but a very disturbing sound that made you want to run from Jeffrey instead of comfort him. As soon as he would begin to cry in the nursery, the nurses quickly shuttled him down to his mother. Within the first day after birth I had a conference with Jeffrey's parents and prepared them for how Jeffrey's cry could interfere with developing a close bonding relationship. I offered suggestions on how to mellow these cries. Jeffrey was to fully room-in with his mother. His cries were to be given an immediate nurturant response. When they took Jeffrey home they were to wear him in a baby sling for at least three hours a day and, if they were comfortable with the arrangement, they were to nap and sleep with Jeffrey. They were to tape-record Jeffrey's cries over a period of two weeks.

An amazing but not unexpected result occurred. By the time Jeffrey's parents brought him into the office for his two-week check, his cries had mellowed considerably. Mother even confessed, "He cries much nicer now!" Since the cry is one of the most powerful enforcers of a strong and early mother-infant attachment, it is important to teach your baby to cry better very early in infancy.

Many babies do not show fussy behavior until around two weeks of age, when the more disturbing cries seem to begin. I call this the "two-week grace period." I suspect that some babies are born potentially fussy but give their care-givers a two-week opportunity to mellow their temperaments. If the babies do not receive the nurturing level they need, the fussing begins. But you can usually spot a high-need baby right after birth—it's as though he looks up and says, "Hi, mom and dad. I am an above-average baby and I need above-average parenting. If you give it to me we're going to get along fine. If you don't, we're going to have a bit of trouble down the line."

Picture the newborn nursery and let's follow the course of a nursery-reared baby and a rooming-in baby to see how early infant care practice can affect the infant's temperament. A nursery-reared baby is lying in his plastic box. He awakens hungry and cries along with 20 other babies in plastic boxes who have all managed to awake each other. A caring nurse, but one who has no biological attachment to the baby, hears the early attachment-promoting cries and responds as soon as time permits. Baby is then taken to the mother with varying degrees of non-urgency. The mother, meanwhile, has missed the opening scene in this biological drama because she was not present in the nursery when her baby first cried. She missed the attachment-promoting beginning of the infant's cry. By the time baby comes to her, his cries have escalated into a sound that disturbs the mother and interferes with her ability to calm her baby. Even though she has a comforting breast to offer the baby, she is so tied up in knots that her milk doesn't arrive, and the baby cries even harder. The mother feels like a failure as the "experts" in the nursery take over. This leads to more separation, more missed cues, more breaks in the attachment between mother and baby, and they leave the hospital as strangers. Baby and mother were out of sync at a biologically sensitive time when they both needed to be with each other.

Contrast the nursery baby with the rooming-in baby. When this baby cries, the mother, because she is right there, hears the attachment-promoting qualities of the baby's cry and gives an immediate nurturant response, before the baby has had a chance to develop the disturbing type of cry. The mother, not the nurse, is the one who hears the opening sounds. These attachment-promoting sounds stimulate her hormonal response, which gives her a biological head start on developing her nurturing abilities. As the pair practice this stimulus-response dialogue over the next day or so, mother learns to read baby's *pre-cry* signals so that when baby awakens, squirms, or grimaces mother knows that the next signal will be a cry. She intervenes and comforts her baby before baby has to cry. Baby soon learns that he does not have to fuss to get his needs met. Mother and baby are in biological harmony: baby fusses less and mother is developing her sensitivity. Nursery-reared babies cry harder, rooming-in babies cry better.

Besides getting this communication system off to the right start in the newborn period, here are some more suggestions in helping your baby develop means of communication other than crying and to develop your sensitivity to reading your baby, creating a communication network in which your baby does not *have* to cry.

Develop a healthy attitude towards your baby's cries. Think of them as a signal to be valued, not a habit to be broken. This starts your crying communication network off on the right note. Your baby's cries are a sign to be responded to, mellowed out and then fine-tuned into better communication skills.

Act, don't think. When you first hear your baby cry, react spontaneously according to the first feeling your intuition prompts. Don't stop and think, "Why is he crying? Is he trying to manipulate me? Will I spoil him?" This type of cry analysis comes much later, after your communication network is well established. It isn't as important to know why your baby is crying as it is simply to respond. Giving an immediate nurturant response to your baby's cry helps to develop your intuition, so that eventually you will better understand why your baby is crying and better trust your intuitive response.

Examine your after-cry feeling. A new mother who had followed the restraint advice of a well-meaning friend shared her feelings with me. "One night when he woke up with his usual demanding cry at 3:00 A.M., I decided to let him cry it out. Boy, was he furious! I'll never do that again, I felt so guilty. His crying was bad for both of us." Parents, especially mothers, are endowed with some internal sensor that feels right when you respond right and feels wrong when you respond wrongly. This feeling is a healthy guilt that lets you know you have violated your internal sensor. Whenever a mother tells me, "My baby's cry doesn't bother me anymore," I red-tag that baby's chart because somewhere down the road mother and baby may have communication problems.

Anticipate baby's need before crying begins. An experienced mother who is very much in harmony with her high-need baby told me, "My baby seldom cries. She doesn't need to." The ultimate in cry-mellowing is to be so tuned in to your baby's cues that she doesn't have to cry to get what she needs.

That old line, "Crying is good for his lungs" is supported by neither common sense nor scientific research. Studies show absolutely no beneficial effect of crying. Actually, crying causes a worrisome increase in baby's heart rate. The oxygen level in baby's blood may be diminished; some may even pass out from prolonged crying. A pediatrician father summed up this bit of misguided advice by saying, "Crying is as good for the lungs as bleeding is for the veins." Another bit of misguided "wisdom" is this: if you pick him up every time he cries, he'll become a whiny child and never stop crying. This is a carryover from an old school of behavior psychology that based its erroneous teachings more on personal opinion than on scientific research. Studies have shown that babies whose cries are promptly attended to early on actually learn to cry and whine less as older infants and toddlers. Some researchers even feel that unattended-to crying may delay a baby's development, perhaps by causing the baby to divert so much energy into learning his own self-soothing skills.

Feed on cue rather than on rigid feeding schedule. Studies have shown that rigid feeding routines lead to excessive and unnecessary fussing. Feeding babies whenever they show signs of hunger prevents initial cries from turning into more disturbing cries. Babies nurse for comfort as well as for nourishment; they should not have to wait until a set time.

6

BABY-WEARING

Organizing the temperament of your baby. Because our fourth child, Hayden, was such a fussy baby and restless sleeper, I have been personally motivated to study why some babies behave this way and what parents can do about it. I have concluded that some babies just come "wired" disorganized and the "treatment" is to organize the temperament of these babies. Specialists in infant development who travel throughout the world studying the temperaments of babies in other cultures have made an interesting observation. Although infants in all cultures fuss and get colic, infants in some cultures definitely cry less, sleep better, and seem to show less fussy behavior. I was interested in this observation and began studying what other cultures do to organize their baby's temperaments.

The main parenting skill practiced in these cultures with less fussy babies is the custom of *wearing the baby*. Baby is carried in a sling-type carrier by mother, father, relatives, and friends during most of the day. A patient of mine just returned from the island of Bali, where she witnessed a ground-touching ceremony. In this culture a baby is carried all day long and put down only to sleep (and then next to the mother). At age six months the baby is ceremoniously put down on the floor to begin freestyle movements. These cultures do not have child psychologists or baby books. Centuries of tradition have simply taught them that babies behave better when they are carried a lot.

At a parenting conference I recently interviewed two

27

mothers from Zambia. They were wearing their babies in attractive home-made slings that were extensions of their gowns. I asked them why mothers in their culture wear their babies. Their response was very simple but insightful: "It's easier for the mother" and "It's good for the baby." Isn't this what we parents want?

How baby-wearing organizes and regulates the baby. A newborn baby comes disorganized. His movements are random and jerky. Many of his cues seem purposeless and hard to decode. His bodily functions, most noticeably his breathing patterns and heart rate, are irregular. In the early months babies seem to waste a lot of energy fussing in order to adjust to life outside the womb. Baby's day-night and feeding patterns are exhaustingly unpredictable. The infant's muscle tone and behavior are often anxiously tense and fluctuating—"One minute he is relaxed and quiet, the next minute he is tense and upset," parents will often report. In the early months one of the most important parental goals is to regulate the baby. Baby-wearing helps parents accomplish this vital function.

Mother's role as a regulator. There has been much research attesting to the value of the mother as a regulator of the baby. During baby-wearing, mother (and father) provide an external regulating system that balances the irregular and disorganizing tendencies of the baby. Picture how these regulating systems work. Mother's rhythmic walk (which baby has been used to for nine months) reminds baby of the womb. This familiar rhythm, which has been imprinted on baby's mind while in the womb, now reappears in the "outside" womb and has a calming effect on the baby. Mother's heartbeat, beautifully regular and familiar, reminds baby of the sounds of the womb as baby places his ear against mother's chest while being worn. Mother's rhythmic respiration is another biological regulator as baby senses her breathing while tummy-to-tummy, chest-to-chest with her. Simply stated, the regular parental rhythms have a balancing effect on the infant's irregular rhythm. One way mother exerts this regulatory effect is by stimulating the regulating hormones in baby's developing adrenal and nervous systems. Researchers have shown that continued mother-infant attachment, which is what baby-wearing provides, stimulates the infant to achieve quicker day-night regulation. They believe that mother's presence exerts a regulatory influence on the baby's adrenal hormones, promoting night sleeping and day waking.

Mother's voice, to which baby is constantly exposed during baby-wearing, has been shown to regulate baby's limb movements. Videoanalysis of an infant's body movements while his mother was talking showed that her infant moved in perfect synchrony with the inflections of mother's speech during her unique "baby talk." These synchronous movements did not occur in response to a stranger's voice. In essence, the mother's rhythmic movements and vocalization "teach" the baby to put more rhythm into his movements, balancing out the usual newborn tendency toward irregular, uncoordinated and purposeless movements.

Baby-wearing exerts a regulatory effect on the infant primarily by its effect on his vestibular system. This tiny system, located behind each ear, is similar to three tiny carpenter's levels—one oriented for side-to-side, another for up-and-down, and a third for back-and-forth motion. When carried, baby moves in all three of these directions; three "levels" all function together to keep the body in balance. Every time you move, the fluid in these "levels" moves against tiny, hairlike filaments that vibrate and send nerve impulses to the muscles of your body to keep you in balance. For example, if you lean too far to one side, the vestibular system signals that you should lean over to the other side to stay in balance. Before birth the baby has a very sensitive vestibular system, which is constantly stimulated because the fetus is in almost continuous motion. Baby-wearing "reminds" the baby of and continues the motion and balance he enjoyed in the womb.

It is easier to understand the care of a high-need baby when you think of his gestation as lasting a full 18 months: nine months inside the womb and at least nine more months outside. During the first nine months mother's primary role is to nourish the baby and to contribute to his physical development. The womb environment regulates baby's sensory and other systems. Birth temporarily disrupts this organization. The more quickly the baby gets outside help with organizing these systems, however, the more easily he adapts to the puzzle of life outside the womb. What may happen if the baby does not have the benefit of being worn during those crucial months when he needs organizing—if he spends most of his time lying in his crib attended to only at dutiful intervals for feeding and comforting? A newborn has an inherent urge to become organized, to fit into his new environment. If left to his own resources without the frequent, and, indeed, almost continuous presence of the mother, the infant develops very disorganized patterns of behavior: colic, fussy cries, jerky movements, self-rocking behavior, anxious thumbsucking, irregular breathing and a lesser quality of sleep. The infant who is forced to self-regulate before his time spends a lot of energy self-calming, wasting valuable energy he could have used to grow and develop. In some babies, fussing and disorganizing behavior is a withdrawal symptom resulting from the loss of the regulatory effects of the attachment to the mother. High-need babies should not be left alone to train themselves to become self-soothers, as some parenting advisers would suggest. This style of detachment parenting is not supported by common sense, experience or medical research. Behavioral research has repeatedly shown that infants exhibit more anxious and disorganized behavior when separated from their mothers. While there is a variety of child-rearing theories, attachment researchers all agree on one thing: in order for a baby's emotional, intellectual, and physiological systems to function optimally, the continued presence of the mother, as during baby-wearing is a necessary regulatory influence.

Current research shows that baby-wearing reduces crying and colic. Parents in my practice commonly report, "As long as I wear him, he's content!" Baby-wearing parents of previously fussy babies relate that their babies seem to forget to fuss. Parents are happier because their babies cry less. Babies are happier because they cry less. Families are happier and I'm happier because finally there seems to be a way to reduce crying in fussy babies. This is why over the past three years parents in our practice always leave the hospital with two baby-care items: a car seat and a baby sling.

Other pediatricians have noticed the effect that carrying babies has on reducing crying. In 1986 Dr. Hunziker and a team of researchers in Montreal reported a study of 99 mother-infant pairs. Half of the mothers were asked to carry their babies for at least three hours a day. In the control, or non-carried, group, parents were asked to position their babies facing a mobile or pictures of a face with baby in a crib, but not to try to calm the baby by increased carrying. The infants who received supplemental carrying cried and fussed 43% less than the non-carried group. The difference in this carrying study was that mothers were encouraged to carry their infants throughout the day regardless of the state of the infant, not just in response to crying. The usual mode of carrying in Western society is to pick up and carry the baby in response to crying after the crying has started.

Baby-wearing reduces crying by its organizing effect on

the baby's vestibular system, as previously described. Vestibular stimulation (e.g., rocking and carrying) has been shown by long experience and detailed research to be the best cry stopper for tiny babies. Vestibular stimulation, as occurs during baby-wearing, soothes baby because it reminds him of the womb, allowing him to click into the pleasant prenatal experiences that were imprinted upon his developing mind. The familiar overcomes the unfamiliar to which baby is now exposed. This lessens baby's anxiety and his need to fuss. Baby is still connected, not "on his own," not left helpless, so there is no reason to panic. Baby's survival is not in jeopardy.

One of the characteristics I have noticed in high-need babies who are carried a lot is that they seem to be very bright. A baby who is carried a lot is intimately involved in his wearer's world. Baby sees what mother or father sees, hears what they hear and in some way feels what they feel. (Mothers will often say, "When I'm upset, he's upset.")

Wearing humanizes baby. Carried babies become more aware of their parents' faces, of their parents' walking rhythm and scent. Baby becomes aware of and learns from the subtle facial expressions and other body language, voice inflections and tones, breath and emotions of the baby-wearer. A parent will relate to the baby much more often just by virtue of the fact that baby is "sitting there right under your nose." Proximity increases interaction and baby is constantly learning how to be human. Carried babies are intimately involved in their parents' world because they participate in what mother and father are doing. A baby "worn" while mom washes dishes, for example, hears, smells, sees, and experiences in depth the adult world. He is more exposed to and involved in what is going on around him. Baby learns much in the arms of a busy person. Cultures the world over have for centuries worn their babies, probably more out of necessity than to stimulate learning. But no doubt these cultures also realize the learning value of this custom of infant care.

Consider the alternative infant-care practice by which baby is separate from the mother most of the day and only picked up and interacted with at dutiful intervals. Life at a distance has no learning value to him. The voices he may hear in another room are not associated with anything happening to him. Because they have no meaning to him, he does not store them. He gets the message that they are not important or worth storing. For the infant who lives alone, normal daily experiences have no learning value for the baby nor bonding value to the mother. Because baby is separate from her, mother does not, as a matter or course, gear her activities and interactions as if the baby were a participating second or third party. At best baby is involved as in a spectator sport rather than a contact sport.

The baby-wearing mother, on the other hand, because she is used to her baby being with her, automatically gears her interactions to include the baby. The baby, in turn, feels that he is included, and feels that he is valuable—a real boost to his emerging self-esteem. Ambient sounds, such as the normal noises of daily activities, may either have learning value to baby or disturb him. If a baby is alone, sounds may frighten him. If a baby is worn, these sounds have learning value. The mother filters out what she perceives unsuitable for the baby and gives the infant an "it's okay" feeling when he is exposed to unfamiliar sounds and experiences.

7

WHY BABIES FUSS

It may help you understand how baby-wearing reduces fussing by understanding why babies fuss in the first place.

Missing the womb. Many babies fuss because they simply miss the womb. Consider for a moment the world of the preborn baby. The womb is a very comfortable home. The environment is just the right temperature. The baby is never cold or hungry, and there isn't even the pain of diaper rash. Baby is lulled constantly by the sounds and movements of his mother. He is in almost constant motion, a free-floating environment free of discomfort. Because the womb environment is so organized, baby feels right. His needs are met consistently and automatically. He does not have to fuss to get what he needs.

Enter birth. This organization is now disrupted. Temperature fluctuates, baby's needs are not consistently and automatically met, and he enters, rather abruptly, from the world of the familiar to that of the unfamiliar. For the first time in his life he must "ask" for what he needs. If he needs to be picked up and held, he fusses; if he needs to be fed he fusses; soon baby learns to fuss in order to alert his caregiving environment to approximate the womb environment as much as possible. It seems as if baby is saying, "Give me back my womb." I sincerely believe that a baby anticipates that he will be held and carried close to mother, as he has been used to for nine months. Could much of the fussy behavior that babies develop during the early weeks of life be the result of this anticipation not being met? The world he expected was not the world he got, and he learns to fuss in order to achieve his expectations. Baby-wearing resembles the womb as closely as is humanly possible and fulfills the style of parenting that baby anticipates. He is close to the warmth of the mother and the sounds he has learned to love. Baby-wearing helps a new baby fit into his environment. It creates a rightness of fit that lessens the need to fuss. Baby is learning to fit into his outside womb as he did the inside womb. We may erroneously regard birth as the end of an assembly line producing a tiny person immediately ready to adapt to his world. It helps if we regard the newborn baby as somewhat *incomplete*. Baby-wearing completes the attachment that baby was used to, giving him a sense of rightness. A baby comes to feel valuable by the way he is treated. Wearing values the baby.

The stimulus barrier is another reason why babies fuss. Ever wonder why some babies can fall asleep and stay asleep at a party or even in a noisy crowd? Most babies are endowed with the ability to selectively block out and adapt to disturbing stimuli. Those with a very effective stimulus barrier are adaptable and not easily upset by noisy crowds. Some high-need babies have a very permeable stimulus barrier and are unable to block out disturbances. The disturbance is translated into fussy behavior. They also fuss in an appeal to their caregivers to provide a stimulus barrier and help them fit into their environment better. Baby-wearing acts as this stimulus barrier, a protective retreat when the outside world is too stimulating. The baby-wearing mother acts as an emotional gatekeeper, selectively filtering out those stimuli that she perceives will upset her baby and exposing him to experiences that she perceives will be pleasant to him. As a result, baby develops a sense of equilibrium between himself and his environment. He fits and does not have to fuss.

Baby-wearing reduces colic. A colicky baby screams

from intense physical discomfort. He draws up his legs onto a tense, gas-filled abdomen and clenches his fists, apparently angry at having this uncontrollable pain. A colicky baby communicates this pain to his parents, who feel helpless in determining its cause. The violent and agonizing quality of the colic cry drives parents to the edge. The cry of a colicky baby occurs in sudden and unexpected oubursts. Bewildered parents will often say, "He seemed perfectly happy and content just a minute ago, and now he's a wreck." In some babies colic may have physical causes (see Key 10). In other babies, I believe colic results when the infant's coping reserves are exhausted because his attempts to fit and adapt into the environment have been unsuccessful.

Colic is something a baby does, not something he has. Colic can be caused by intestinal disturbances, but in most cases we contribute colic to the wrong end of the baby. It often seems more like a temperamental and neurodevelopmental problem than strictly an intestinal problem. I feel that the colicky baby belongs to the whole spectrum of fussy or high-need babies. They come wired with a supersensitive, intense, disorganized, and slow-to-adapt temperament. Rather then fuss all the time, the colicky baby concentrates his fussiness toward the end of the day as if he has stored it all up for the evening blast.

Is colic preventable? I find it very interesting that colic usually does not begin until after the second week of life. Could it be that the infant is giving us a two-week "grace period" to help him get organized and adjust to life outside the womb? Wearing the baby can prevent his system from going to disequilibrium and disorganization.

There is a tendency in our culture to view the newborn as a separate person from the mother, but the newborn doesn't feel that way. I believe that high-need babies need to be worn by their mothers and fathers almost continuously for the first week or two after birth and generally cared for in an organized, predictable, womblike environment. If these infants do not get what they need and expect, they react with the behavior we call colic, which may be nothing more than the desperation and anger of a baby who is not fitting well into his environment. I believe this may be the contributing factor in some but not all colicky babies.

Even babies who are worn from day one get colic; then a medical cause should be suspected. The position that baby assumes during baby-wearing will often alleviate even some of the medical causes of colic, such as regurgitation of stomach acids into the upper esophagus, a sensation like adult "heartburn," and gas retention in the stomach. One of the most experienced baby-wearing mothers in my practice feels that wearing her baby after feeding promotes "digestive organization," and that gentle motion and closeness to the mother enhance intestinal function. I share this mother's belief. Perhaps this is similar to the instinct mother cats have to lick their kittens' abdomens after feeding.

Even when colic is due to a medical rather than a behavioral cause, those parents who wear their babies are better able to cope with the colicky behavior. The closeness they achieve while wearing their babies creates a *sensitivity* in these parents, causing them to be exquisitely responsive to their infants' needs. Baby-wearing parents also learn to anticipate and avoid the triggers of colicky behavior.

Baby-wearing is especially valuable in preventing so-called "evening colic"—the baby who absolutely disintegrates around six to seven o'clock in the evening, a time surviving parents have labeled as "happy hour." (A father once asked me what quality a parent must have to survive the colicky baby; I responded, "a sense of humor."). It could be that baby spends most of his day trying to compensate and fit into his environment and using his own semisuccessful self-soothing techniques. By the end of the day he is so exhausted by trying to fit in that he bitterly decompensates into colicky behavior. Baby-wearing during the day in effect compensates and helps baby organize the day, therefore relieving evening colic. The tension that would have built up during the day and would need to be released at night in colic is not there because baby-wearing has done its part to help the baby fit.

Baby-wearing helps babies cry better and parents cope better. Because a baby-wearing mother is so close to her infant, she anticipates baby's pre-cry signals and meets the baby's needs even before he has to cry. Both the baby and the mother learn non-crying modes of communication. Even if mother occasionally misses the opening cue and baby does cry, because the pair is so close, the mother gives an immediate nurturant response during the attachment part of the crying curve (see Key 3 for analysis of baby's cry) and does not require the cry to intensify. In effect, baby learns to cry better. Mothers, please remember it is not your fault that your baby cries, nor is it always your job not to allow baby to cry. Sometimes the best you can do is not to let your baby cry alone, and to create a secure environment that lessens a baby's need to cry. Baby-wearing helps you do this.

8

~~~~~~

WHAT IS COLIC?

A t least 24% of babies are labeled "fussy" at some time during the early months. About half of these babies will fuss to the degree that they are labeled as colicky. The difference between the terms "colicky" and "fussy" is primarily that of cause and degree, although there is a large overlap between these two types of babies. I refer to a screaming baby as "colicky" if the cries have primarily physical causes and as "fussy" if baby's cries stem primarily from baby's temperament. If you are wondering whether or not you have a colicky baby, you probably don't. The cries of a colicky baby are so penetrating and shattering that this baby leaves no doubt in the mind of sympathetic caregivers that he is truly in agony.

Colic is not a disease; it is syndrome having a number of signs and symptoms that give the picture of a very uncomfortable baby and create havoc in the home. A colicky baby is one who screams from intense physical discomfort, drawing his legs up onto a gas-filled abdomen. But he seems completely well between the colicky episodes.

The paroxysmic nature of the colicky baby's cry, occurring in sudden and unexpected outbursts, is in contrast to the cries of fussy babies, who fuss all day. In contrast to fussy babies, who may be difficult to handle most of the day, most colicky babies are relatively easy to handle when they are not having colicky periods. One mother told me, "He seems like two different babies, Dr. Jekyll and Mr. Hyde." On the outside, colicky babies are the picture of good health. They tend to eat more and grow faster than non-colicky babies. The thriving appearance of the colicky baby often causes onlookers to remark, "My, what a healthy looking baby, you're so lucky." Worn-out mothers respond, "You should have seen us a few hours ago."

The "ouch" sign is characteristic of the colicky baby's painful cries. When you look at the baby's face and whole body, the most disturbing feature of the colic cry is the total body language that accompanies it: flinging of arms and legs, clenched fists, facial grimaces, a wide-open mouth, furrowed brow, anger, tenseness and a hard tummy. The baby's arms are clenched tightly close to his chest and his knees are drawn up so tightly that they nearly bump his bloated abdomen. Periodically during these attacks the infant may throw out his arms, stiffen his back, arch his neck and dart out his legs, a move resembling a frantically executed back dive. Babies often fall into a deep sleep after the colicky episode is over.

The violent and agonizing quality of the colic cry and the unrelenting nature of colic attacks is what drives parents to the edge. Colicky spells may last a few minutes to a few hours, with occasional pauses before the next storm breaks. By some perverse quirk of justice, colic seldom occurs in the morning, when parents and infants are well rested. It usually occurs in late afternoon or early evening, when parental reserves are lowest. The predominance of evening colic suggests that baby has been storing up bodily tension all day long and then relieves this tension in his evening blast. The difference between a colicky baby and simply a crying or fussy baby is usually a difference of degree. Doctors have come up with a uniform description of colic so that a baby can truly be determined colicky if he meets the following criteria:

- Paroxysms of inconsolable crying without any identifiable physical causes.
- Begins within the first three weeks.
- Lasts three hours per day, three days per week, and continues for at least three weeks.
- Occurs in otherwise healthy, thriving infants. These are arbitrary figures and vary widely from baby to baby and from day to day in the same baby.

9

WHY COLIC?

T he term "colic" means an acute, sharp pain in the abdomen. Because the pain was once thought to be caused by gas in the colon, it was labeled "colic." But in fact it is seldom an intestinal problem and is seldom caused by "gas." There are medical causes of colic (see Key 14). The colicky symptoms in many babies are due to an overall tension release from a generally upset baby. Two of the most popular myths about colic are that it is caused by either tense parents or "gas."

The tense mother—tense baby syndrome. Parents do not cause their baby's colic, they respond to it. Colicky behavior in an infant is sometimes unjustly blamed on the parent. It is felt that the mother tranfers her own anxiety to the baby and the baby reacts with colic. In most cases of colic this just isn't true. Colic occurs in babies of accepting, easygoing mothers as well as in babies whose mothers are more prone to be anxious. This is an important point because the behavior of a baby is often unjustly used as an index of the "goodness" of the mother. It is true that mothers vary widely in their coping abilities and that colic, like any stress that is not quickly dealt with, can be prolonged and reinforced by the mother's tension. Some studies have shown absolutely no correlation between the personality of the mother and colicky behavior in the baby. Other studies have shown that mothers who score high on the anxiety portion of personality tests are more likely to have colicky babies. Mothers who are tense, anxious, and depressed during their pregnancy are also more likely to have colicky babies. But in general, most studies suggest no correlation between a mother's disposition and her having a colicky baby.

The emotional makeup of the mother has more influence on her handling of the colicky baby than it does on the cause of the colic. A tense baby doesn't settle well in tense arms. It is true that tense parents can aggravate a baby's colic, but it is very hard to relax with a screaming baby. Parental tension is aggravated by the lack of answers as to why the baby has colic; no one, neither the pediatrician nor the wise grandmother, can say why a baby is colicky. This has a significant effect on the parents' sympathy for the colicky baby. Physical causes of pain have a way of eliciting sympathy. It is much easier to comfort a person who is hurting when there is a readily identifiable medical cause for the hurt. While unknown causes can bring out a sympathetic response from parents, they also run the risk of creating reactions like, "I'm being manipulated" or "I've been had." These feelings may add a bit of restraint to the caregiver's nurturing responses, especially if they are reinforced by well-meaning advisors who admonish the mother that she will spoil her baby if she responds every time he cries.

Smoking and colic. There is a higher incidence of colic in infants whose mothers smoke. The same study also showed a higher incidence of colic when the father smoked, leading the researchers to conclude that the effects were the result of smoke in the home environment rather than a direct transfer of chemicals through the mother's milk. Not only are smoking mothers more likely to have colicky babies, but their coping abilities may be lessened. Recent studies have shown that mothers who smoke have lower levels of prolactin, the "mothering hormone."

Birth events and colic. The incidence of colic is higher in infants who are the product of complicated and stressful births and who experience a lot of mother-baby separation after birth. This goes along with the general tendency for infants to be fussy if they had a rough start and were separated from their mothers.

"Oh, she's just full of gas!" In the long and often fruitless search for the cause of colic, gas has often been labeled as the culprit. During colicky periods, the infant's tummy does seem to be more distended, and she passes a lot of flatus. But X-ray studies cast some doubt on the theory that intestinal gas is the culprit in colic. Abdominal X-rays of non-colicky babies frequently reveal a lot of distention of the intestines with gas, but the infants do not seem to be uncomfortable. X-rays taken during and after colic crying spells showed no gas during the crying episodes but a lot of gas afterwards. Air is gulped and swallowed during crying. Distention of the intestines by gas may be the *result* rather than the *cause* of colicky crying. This is another reason why a prompt response to crying is important. Avoiding the crying episode may lessen the amount of air the baby swallows, thus decreasing the amount of intestinal gas and shortening the duration of the colic cry. Those infants who are truly gassy babies should be trained to cry better. (see Key 5 for teaching your baby to cry better).

Evening colic. One reason that I believe that colic is a neurodevelopmental or even a hormonal problem is that it occurs most often in the evening. If colic were caused by medical problems, such as allergies, why would baby be colicky for only three hours a day? While no one completely understands why colic occurs mainly in the evening, consider the following possible explanations.

Exhausted parental reserves. By late afternoon or evening, most mothers are worn out by their babies' incessant demands. Even the most time-honored comforter, mother's breast, may not measure up to expectations at the end of the day. Levels of fat and protein in breast milk are lowest toward evening, so that nursing may be less satisfying for the baby at this time. Many mothers report a diminished milk supply toward evening. Mothers also experience hormonal changes in the evening. Prolactin, which I call the "perseverance hormone" is highest during sleep and in the morning hours. The blood level of cortisone—which may also affect maternal coping—is lowest around 6:00 P.M.

Colic may be a disturbance in daily biologic rhythms. The body has daily fluctuations in temperature, hormonal concentration, and sleep patterns. Biological peaks and valleys occur throughout each 24-hour period. Two important hormones, cortisone and growth hormone, are highest in the early morning hours and lowest in the evening hours. In the first few months of a baby's life, the daily fluctuations in hormones are very disorganized. By four to six months of age, the pattern becomes more consistent. Around the same age a baby's sleep patterns become more organized and colic subsides. Could there be a cause and effect relationship between the organization of these hormonal patterns and the disappearance of colic?

Hormonal disturbances. In addition to disorganization of biological rhythms, could colic be the result of hormonal disturbances? I have always wondered if there could be a deficiency of the hormone that would normally calm the baby toward the end of the day, or an excess of another hormone that upsets the baby in the evening hours. There are a few studies that lend support to this possibility. Progesterone is a hormone that can have calming and sleep-inducing effects.

45

A baby receives progesterone from the placenta at birth. The calming effect of this maternal progesterone wears off in a week or two, and it could be that colic begins if the infant does not produce enough progesterone on his own. Studies of progesterone levels in colicky babies have shown mixed results, with some but not all showing low levels in colicky babies. It is interesting that these studies also show that breastfed babies have higher levels of progesterone, a possible reason why colic occurs less in breastfed infants.

Prostaglandin, a hormone causing strong contractions of intestinal muscle, has also been implicated in colic. One study showed that infants develop colicky symptoms when given prostaglandin therapeutically to treat their heart disease. The increased incidence of colic in infants who were the products of unusually stressful delivery may also lend support to the theory that colic is due to a disturbance in biological rhythm and hormonal problems. I suspect that with technology's new abilities to measure hormones in babies, we will soon discover the effect of a stressful birth and postpartum course on the later behavior of some infants.

Plan ahead for evening colic. Putting all these theories together, I suspect that colic is the result of many physiological, temperamental, and environmental causes that overwhelm a baby's immature coping skills. When I witness a colicky episode I can't help but feel that something physical and chemical is going on within that baby. He is not just upset, he hurts! I want to reach for some magic medicine that will bring instant relief to this helpless little person, yet I know full well that I cannot offer treatment if I do not know the cause. In light of the present knowledge about colic, the best anyone can do is comfort the baby and minimize the factors that may contribute to his fussiness. If you have a baby whose colic occurs primarily in the evening (as most babies' does), plan ahead for this stressful time by completing all of your busy and energy-draining chores earlier in the day. Prepare the evening meal in advance. Parents of colicky babies get used to casseroles that can be made ahead of time. Take care of housework and other necessary duties earlier in the day and avoid chores and commitments that will sap your energy during the colicky evening times.

A 4:00 P.M. nap may be lifesaving. Lie down with your baby and nurse him off to sleep around this time. Mother gets a rest and a boost in her prolactin levels, and she recharges her energy system in preparation for the evening colic. Baby's system also gets a rest at this crucial time before the colic comes. Mothers in my practice report that late afternoon quiet time minimizes the frequency and severity of the evening colic, and at least increases their ability to cope when their baby does have colic.

When will colic stop? Most colic occurs around two weeks of age, reaches its maximum severity between six and eight weeks and usually gradually subsides between six and eight months. In a study of 100 colicky babies, the colic had disappeared in 50% by three months and in 90% by six months. In only 1% of these babies did the colic last until one year of age. In my experience, colic that persists beyond three to four months is likely to be caused by a medical problem, such as milk intolerance.

Colic occurs at an age and stage of an infant's life when he can do the least to comfort and amuse himself. During the first three months, babies are almost totally dependent on their caregivers for stimulation. The severity of colic seems to lessen along with the infant's development. I believe the reason that colic begins to subside at around three months of age is that by this time babies can finally see clearly and are attracted by the visual delights and distractions around them. They can begin doing things with their hands and learning self-soothing techniques such as finger sucking, eye contact, and waving their arms and legs to let off steam. Also, around three months of age most babies show an increased central nervous system maturity, as evidenced by gradual organization of their sleep patterns. By the time baby is two or three months old, parents have become more adept at soothing techniques.

Understanding, comforting, and coping with the colicky baby (if done with proper support and consultation) will bring you closer to your baby and enhance parent-infant bonding. Nothing brings out ingenious comforting skills like a colicky baby. Parents, take heart—like most problems in infancy, colic too will pass.

10

MEDICAL CAUSES OF FUSSINESS AND COLIC

While many babies are colicky because of their inability to adjust to life outside the womb, there are medical reasons why some babies scream.

Food allergies as the cause of colic. Infants whose colic is caused by food allergies are known as "allergic crampers." In the majority of colicky infants there is no relationship between type of milk and colic; the search for the "right formula" is often fruitless. Most studies show no difference in colic incidence between breastfed and formula-fed babies. In my experience, however, breastfeeding mothers often exhibit better coping skills. Recent studies have implicated milk and cow's milk–based formulas as a cause of colic. For this reason, your doctor may choose to substitute a soy formula. But even soy formula can cause colic. Approximately 35% of infants who are allergic to cow's milk–based formulas will also be allergic to soy milk–based formulas. A recent discovery is that cow's-milk allergens may enter the milk of a breastfeeding mother and irritate the baby's intestines, causing colic. This is why it is often worthwhile to try a dairy-free diet in treating the colicky infant of a breastfeeding mother.

Do gassy foods produce gassy babies? There is recent focus on the foods that a breastfeeding mother eats as affecting the intestines and behavior of her baby. I have found a discrepancy between mothers' testimonies and nutritional science. Nutritionists believe there is no scientific rationale for thinking that the food the mother eats gets into her breast milk and produces gas in the baby (except studies documenting cow's-milk allergens entering mother's breast milk). But occasionally a mother will tell me that she notices colicky symptoms in her baby within a few hours of eating certain foods. The foods most commonly reported as causing colicky symptoms are:

- Raw vegetables: broccoli, cabbage, onions, green peppers, cauliflower
- Chocolate
- Eggs
- Shellfish
- Nuts
- Citrus fruits
- Synthetic vitamins (either mother's or baby's)

If you taste your milk regularly, you may be able to identify which foods change its flavor. Several mothers have told me that they have noticed a change in the taste of their milk after they have indulged in certain foods. The taste also coincided with a colicky period in their babies. Recent studies have also implicated cow's-milk allergies as a cause of frequent night waking. If milk allergy is the expected cause of colic, more often there are other allergic signs: a raised, red, sandpaperlike rash on baby's face and other areas of the skin, diarrhea, occasional vomiting, sleep disturbances, runny noses, frequent ear infections, and a red, burnt-looking bottom. If you suspect milk allergies, try the following:

1. If you are breastfeeding, go on a dairy-free diet for at least a week, preferably two. If your baby's colicky symptoms disappear, reintroduce dairy into your diet and see if the same colicky symptoms reappear. If they do, then dairy products may be a contributing factor.
2. If you are formula feeding, switch to a soy for-

mula. If not, switch to a hypoallergenic formula prescribed by your doctor. In these formulas, potentially allergenic proteins are predigested. But some of these formulas are very expensive and poor-tasting. Do not use them without your doctor's advice.

Ear infections may cause colicky behavior. Signs that this may be the case are: baby seems to be in pain while lying down, but not while sitting up; he has associated cold symptoms such as a runny nose, draining eyes, and low-grade fever; and he suffers sleep disturbances. A thorough examination of your baby's ears should be part of a colic checkup.

The pediatric regurgitation syndrome (also called gastrointestinal reflux) is a recent discovery as a medical cause of colic. Normally when food goes down your baby's esophagus into his stomach, the stomach then contracts, pushing the already-present food down into the intestines. In some babies the junction of the esophagus and the stomach does not work properly, so when the stomach contracts, some of the food is pushed back up into the esophagus and even out the mouth. Along with this food come irritating stomach acids, which may irritate the esophaghus and produce a feeling of what adults would call "heartburn." Signs that reflux may be contributing to colic are: frequent spitting up after eating; colicky episodes shortly after eating; frequent night waking as if in severe pain; and colic that is just not going away. (Most nonmedical causes of colic disappear by three to six months of age.) The proper diagnosis of reflux is very involved and expensive, often requiring X-rays and the insertion of a tube down the baby's esophagus to measure stomach acids. If this is the case, however, medical treatment is remarkably effective at alleviating the reflux and associated discomfort.

Urinary tract infections. One of the most serious hidden causes of colic is a urinary tract infection. These infections are subtle; they do not begin as quickly and severely as ear infections, and they can last several weeks before they are detected. Urinary tract infections can cause kidney damage if untreated. I believe that all fussy, colicky babies (especially females) should have at least three urinalyses. When making an appointment for a fussy baby consultation, ask the doctor's assistant to mail you three urine bags so you can bring in specimens on or before the day of your appointment.

Skin rashes may also be a cause of colic. Eczema, allergic-type rashes and diaper rashes may be the culprit. Sudden outbursts of screaming may be caused by a sore bottom. The type of diaper rash that is particularly distressing is the raw, burnlike rash caused by acid stools during diarrhea. A baking soda bath (one tablespoon in a couple of inches of water in baby's bathtub) may soothe the diaper rash caused by acid stools.

Constipation may be a hidden cause of colic. In the early months a baby's stools, especially those of a breastfed infant, should be loose, soft and frequent, averaging two to three a day. Around three or four months some babies will normally have only one bowel movement a day, and some normally every two or three days without any apparent problems. If your baby strains a lot to have a bowel movement, and if the stool seems hard, accompanied by a few drops of rectal bleeding and a tense, gas-filled abdomen, suspect constipation. Your doctor will advise you how to treat this.

11

GETTING HELP FROM YOUR DOCTOR

Colic communication tips. Since most colic occurs outside of doctors' office hours, most baby doctors do not have the privilege of witnessing a colicky attack. When seeking professional help for your colicky or fussy baby, be honest with your doctor about two important points: how much the colic bothers your baby and how much it bothers you. Here are some things you'll need to tell the doctor when discussing your baby's colic problems. Think about them ahead of time and make a list to take with you to the doctor's office:

- When the colic episodes start, how often they occur, how long they last.
- The time of day and the circumstances around which they occur (at home, with caregivers other than mother, when the family is busy).
- What seems to turn the colicky episodes on and what turns them off.
- Where you feel the baby's pain is coming from; what his face, abdomen and extremities look like.
- A description of the cry.
- Details about feeding: breast or bottle, frequency, swallowing, do you hear your baby gulping air?
- Nature of your baby's bowel movements (easy or straining, soft or hard, how frequent).
- How much he passes gas.
- Spitting up: how often after feeding, how much force.

- What baby's bottom looks like: a persistent diaper rash or a red, burnt-looking bottom suggests some sort of food intolerance.
- What you have tried to do for the colicky episodes, what worked and what didn't.
- What your diagnosis or suspicions are.

Be sure to tell your doctor what effect the colic is having on the whole family. I have discovered that it is not uncommon for mothers to open a conversation by telling me, "Our whole family is falling apart—me, my baby, and my marriage." Don't hesitate to let yourself go during an office visit. This gets the point across that your baby's colic bothers you. Some mothers will minimize the severity of the colic and the effect of the baby's behavior on their coping abilities because of their underlying feeling that they are ineffective as mothers because their babies are colicky. This simply is not true. If your doctor is unable to witness one of these colicky episodes, it may help to make a "distress tape," a recording of one of the baby's crying jags. I find it difficult, though, to truly appreciate a cry from the sound only; there is so much that body language can tell you about the level of the baby's distress. If you really want to get the point across and you have the equipment (or can rent it), have your husband make a videotape of you and your baby during a colicky episode so that your counselor can truly witness a mother-infant pair in distress. Some parents find it very therapeutic to sit back and analyze a series of tapes of crying episodes as their infant gets older. As they look back, parents are often amazed at the complete turnabout in the baby's personality. As they look at some of the distress tapes they often exclaim, "We've come a long way, baby!"

I find it particulary helpful to have parents keep some sort of a diary that lists the activity of the infant on one side of the page and the time of day and activity of the rest of the family on the other. You'll be surprised at correlations you'll discover. For example, I've found that typical colic seldom awakens the baby during the night. Pain that awakens babies from sleep is more likely to have a physical than an emotional cause.

If possible, both mother and father should attend the office visit. The presence of the father keeps mother honest. Mothers may sometimes play down how much their crying baby upsets them. They fear that such a revelation will shatter their perfect-mother image in the eyes of their pediatrician. Fathers may also more readily volunteer how the fussy baby is affecting the overall dynamics of the family. One family came in for colic counseling with me and I really didn't appreciate the severity of the problem until the father volunteered, "I had a vasectomy last week; we'll never go through this again." I got the picture. (Three years later this father underwent a surgical reversal and they are now the parents of another colicky baby, though their coping abilities have definitely matured and they are happy for a second chance).

12

^^

CRY STOPPERS
THAT WORK

Besides wearing your baby a lot, the most valuable of soothing techniques, the following are a list of time-tested methods of settling the fussy baby.

1. **The colic dance.** I have watched mothers and fathers of colicky babies dancing around my office trying to soothe their little ones. One by one the tense babies drift off to sleep and melt into the arms of the parents. Every mother and father who has coped with a colicky baby has developed a unique rhythm, a dance motivated by love and desperation that keeps going until either the fusser or the dancer wears down. While each dance movement is as unique as a fingerprint, there are some common elements that I have observed among all experienced dancers. They hold the baby firmly, with a relaxed "I'm in charge" grasp and with as much skin-to-skin contact as possible. The experienced dancer usually oscillates gently back and forth, alternating side-to-side and up-and-down motions. There is a lot of bending and straightening of the knees as if walking and bending in slow motion. The most successful rhythms are about 70 beats per minute (which corresponds to the pulse of uterine blood flow to which the baby has grown accustomed before birth). Gentle humming usually ac-

companies this dance. It sounds as if the mother is trying to approximate as closely as possible the sounds of the womb.

Fathers are particularly resourceful in developing their own type of colic carry. The one that has worked best for me is to drape our baby stomach down over my forearm, her head in the crook of my elbow and the legs straddling my hand. I grasp the diaper area firmly and my forearm presses on the baby's tense abdomen. As I dance around carrying our tense baby, it is rewarding to feel her body language when her abdomen softens and her arms dangle limply from her sides as she drifts off into a deep sleep.

Another favorite dance is the *neck nestle*. Baby snuggles her head into the groove between my jaw and chest. My jawbone drapes gently over her head and my voicebox (the front of my neck) presses against her head. Tiny babies hear not only with their eardrums, but with the vibrations of their skullbones. Sing something very monotonous and droning, like "Ol' Man River," and your baby should drift comfortably off to sleep. This neck nestle dance works much better for fathers because of the lower pitch and high vibrations of the male voice.

Try dancing with your baby in the bent-forward position. Some high-need babies tend to stiffen their muscles and arch their backs, and do not cuddle easily into the above-mentioned colic dance position. Other babies like to see while being carried, so they do not cuddle at their mother's breast or in the father's neck-nestle position. You can relax this kind of baby by carrying her in a bent-forward position. Press baby's back against your chest and cradle baby in your arms beneath her thighs. When you bend baby's hips and legs upward, she tends to relax her entire back, becoming less of an archer. If your arms give out, you can carry your baby in the baby sling in the facing-forward position—called the kangaroo carry. Some babies prefer a lot of eye contact as you sing and dance with them; others like to be held a foot away from your face with one hand firmly under the bottom and the other firmly on the back. You can then bounce the baby rhythmically, fast or slow, hard or smoothly. This is a good way to get baby to stop crying before going on to his favorite snuggling position. It is especially effective if you can make eye contact and croon baby's name. Don't feel distraught if occasionally your baby does not respond to your comforting dance yet responds when an experienced friend cuts in. Some grandmothers have a very calming way of moving babies. I suspect that it is the softness of the abundant adipose tissue in most grandmothers that babies like to nestle against.

You can develop a colic dance with your preborn baby. Some mothers of large families can often predict the temperament of the baby by its activity in the womb. Mothers who have calmed their agitated preborn babies by songs and dances during pregnancy find that the same songs and dances often work after birth.

2. **The warm fuzzy** works especially well for fathers. Drape the bare-skinned but diapered baby over your bare chest. Place baby's ear over your

heartbeat. The rhythm of your heart combined with the rhythm of your breathing movements plus firm, rhythmic patting on the baby's back will usually soothe both members of this pair back to sleep. In my experience, the warm fuzzy works best in the first three months; older babies squirm too much to lie quietly on dad's chest.

3. **Abdominal relaxation techniques.** Sometimes warm and gentle pressure on the abdomen helps soothe a colicky baby. Place baby tummy down on a half-filled warm water bottle that you have covered with a towel to protect baby's skin. Letting him fall asleep stomach down on a cushion with his legs dangling over the edge causes some soothing pressure to be applied to his belly. Some babies enjoy dad's large, warm hand pressing gently on their tummies. The palms should be over the navel and the fingers and thumb should encircle baby's abdomen. Sometimes inserting a glycerine suppository into the baby's rectum with one hand while kneading baby's abdomen with the other will decompress a gas-filled abdomen.

4. **Motion soothes.** While stillness is a way of life for some babies, for the high-need baby motion is what it's all about. As you grow with your restless baby you will discover amazing motion sources for calming him. Here are a few of these time-tested favorites:

• A mechanical swing will often calm the fussy baby and give parents a few minutes of much-needed rest. These devices are usually set to swing around 60 beats per minute; some have accompanying lullabies. Some infants will not settle while in swings because they provide only a back-and-forth motion.

Homemade hammocklike swings often work better because they allow a wider, more circular motion.

- One mother in my practice placed her baby in a car seat and strapped baby and car seat on top of an automatic dryer. It worked.
- Trampolines—the father of a high-need baby recently told me that he is able to calm his baby by dancing rhythmically on a small home trampoline.
- Riding on the freeway is most effective. After baby falls asleep (this usually takes at least 20 minutes), keep him in the car seat and carry him into the house; let him sleep as long as possible still in the seat.
- Things that move rhythmically and have a consistent, monotonous motion often soothe a fussy baby:
  - Revolving ceiling fan
  - Waves on a beach
  - Shower—place baby in an infant seat in the bathroom and let him watch you take a shower
  - Waterfall
  - Pendulum of a grandfather clock
  - Trees swaying in the wind
  - A metronome
- Playing tick-tock has worked for our babies. Hold your baby upside down by the feet and sway him back and forth like the pendulum of a clock, approximately 60 strokes per minute.
- Beach balls are especially helpful for the older tense baby, beginning at four to six months. Drape baby tummy down over a beach ball and gradually roll it back and forth and side to side as you hold baby's back with one hand.

13

INFANT MASSAGE

Infant massage is becoming quite an art for untensing the restless baby. There are certified infant massage instructors in every major city. Your childbirth education class or local hospital should be able to provide the names of several. We found it very helpful to have an infant massage instructor come to our home for a one-hour demonstration of techniques for soothing our fussy baby. You can also purchase books and videotapes to learn the technique. One good title on the subject is *Infant Massage* by Vimala Schneider McClure, Bantam Books, New York, 1989. The essentials of infant massage are:

- Always massage in a warm, quiet, draft-free room. If possible, take advantage of the warm sun by placing baby near a sunlit window. During the summer, try this in a park or on a beach with the sound of water nearby.
- Get comfortable yourself. You can sit on the floor with baby in front of you on a pillow or blanket, with your legs stretched out alongside your baby and your baby's legs between yours. Or you can sit cross-legged, placing baby in the cradle of your legs facing you.
- Cold-pressed fruit and/or vegetable oils, enhanced with vitamin E and unscented.
- In the beginning be very soft and gentle, gradually increasing the firmness of your touch as you and your baby begin to enjoy this ritual. Make all of your strokes long, slow, and rhythmic, with just enough pressure to be comfortable but stimulating.
- When you are relaxed, focused, and ready to begin, remove

your baby's clothing. As you do, tell him it's massage time and give him a special "cue" that you are about to start. Pour a small amount of massage oil into your palm and rub both hands together.

- If your baby appears stiff and tense, add the technique of touch relaxation while massaging him. Take your baby's legs gently in your hands and rhythmically move the legs in a bicycle motion, repeating the word "relax" in a soft voice over and over. You can do the same touch relaxation to all parts of your baby's tense body. Eventually baby will associate your movements, your soft tone of voice and the term "relax" with the cue to relax her own body. A properly performed infant massage actually relaxes both baby and parent. Babies are very sensitive to every nuance of your touch and feelings. A tense baby being massaged by a tense person will dilute the relaxing nature of the massage.

- In our babies we have found that infant massage works best toward the late afternoon. Most colicky babies will have their worst periods in late afternoon or early evening. A late-afternoon massage ritual helps relieve tension before it stores up and becomes a colicky episode. Babies get used to and look forward to this ritual. We would use the same towel or lambskin in the same place on the floor near a warm, sunlit window. As soon as we set the baby down on the familiar massage pad in the familiar location he knew that the beautiful art of hands-on communication was soon to follow.

The "I love you" technique of abdominal massage. Imagine a large "U" upside down on baby's abdomen. This is the large intestine or colon along which the gas must pass, beginning on baby's right (your left), moving across to his middle and down his left side until it exits through the rectum. By firmly and deeply massaging with your flattened fingers in a circular motion you can move gas pockets along this path. You can use the "I love you" method: Start with a single downward stroke for the "I" on baby's left side. This will move gas down and out of the last one-third of the colon. Then do the upside down "L" (the number 7 as you look at it) for the "Love,'" moving gas along the middle segment and down baby's left side. Finally do the whole upside down "U" for the "You" as you stroke again along baby's right side across the middle segment and down the left side. Baby must be relaxed for this massage to work, as a tense abdomen will resist the motion of your hands. Try it in a warm bath together or after some other comforting treatments. If you use the abdominal massage technique while immersing your baby's tummy in warm water, bubbles may appear in the water as your baby passes the gas. We call this the "bubble bath."

Instead of waiting for your baby to become colicky, I advise beginning a daily ritual of infant massage within the first week after birth. Learning to untense your baby before colic-producing tension builds up may lessen the chances of your baby becoming colicky.

14

MEDICATIONS FOR COLIC

In my experience drug treatment for colic seldom works, but parents and doctors are willing to try anything for the truly colicky baby.

Antispasmodics (e.g. dicyclomine) are prescription drugs that relax the smooth muscle of the intestines. One-half to one teaspoon of this medicine given a half hour before the usual colic time may offer some relief if your doctor suspects intestinal spasms as the cause of the colic.

Antiflatulants (e.g., simethicone drops) are prescription drugs that work by lessening the formation of gas in the intestines. Some parents have reported that acidophilus, basically a yogurt culture, also seems to lessen intestinal gas. It is available in liquid form in health food stores. Give baby a dose of one milliliter with feedings during the colicky times of the day.

Herbal teas (chamomile and fennel) sometimes have a soothing effect on babies. Place one-half teaspoon of tea in a pot with one cup of boiling water. Cover and steep for five to ten minutes. A few teaspoons of this warm tea may help baby feel better.

Glycerine suppositories (baby-size rectal suppositories) may help expel some stool and gas during a straining episode if baby is constipated. These suppositories resemble tiny rockets. Insert the suppository about an inch or so into baby's rectum and hold the buttocks together for a few minutes to allow it to dissolve.

Medical remedies not suggested. Sedatives such as phenobarbital are not proven to be effective in lessening colic; in many instances they have a paradoxical effect and make a fussy baby even fussier. Anticholinergic drugs (containing belladonna) are also advertised for colic, but both their safety and effectiveness are questionable. Some infants have suffered respiratory problems from these drugs. They should not be used without a doctor's advice.

A word of caution. Beware of colic remedies that have not been proven to be both safe and effective. Worn-out parents are particularly vulnerable to any promise of relief, but always check with your doctor before giving your child any drug for colic.

What about sleeping medications? I have one set of criteria for prescribing sleeping medications for the restless baby: The parents ask for them. Doctors are reluctant to prescribe sleeping medications and parents are reluctant to give them. Because of this natural reluctance I have found that if parents have reached the exhausted state where they ask for a sleeping medication, it is worth a trial. When used under the direction of a physician, it will be safe though probably only marginally effective.

Consider sleeping medications only if: 1) you have tried all the natural methods of nighttime parenting and nothing is working; 2) the family is falling apart from stress and fatigue and you are becoming a less effective daytime parent because of your frequent night waking; 3) you are not enjoying your baby in particular or motherhood in general; or 4) in extreme cases when child abuse seems imminent. In these cases one to three nights' use of a sleep medication seems appropriate.

More than three nights may be habit forming for both baby and mother. I teach parents not to rely on sleeping medications but to continue to use all the natural sleep-inducing methods of intuitive nighttime parenting. Also remember that most sleeping medications do not induce normal sleep, may interfere with the usual sleep stages and may impair function the following day. In my experience and in those of sleep researchers, the safest and most effective sleep-inducing drug for infants and children is chloral hydrate. Ask your doctor about this prescription medication. Barbiturates and anti-histamines often have the opposite effects in infants, winding them up instead of winding them down.

The most effective "medicine" for soothing the fussy baby comes out of the parent's heart, not out of the drugstore. It is wise to consider colic not as a disease to be treated but as a person to be comforted.

15

FEEDING THE
FUSSY BABY

Fussy babies tend to be fussy feeders. They often resist scheduling, like to feed during the night, and are sensitive to certain foods. I hope these keys to feeding the high-need baby will help you enjoy the special interaction that feeding time should offer.

Breast or bottle: does it make a difference? Breastfeeding is clearly better for fussy babies—and for their mothers, because it helps achieve the two goals of mellowing the temperament of the baby and improving the sensitivity of the mother. Breastfeeding eliminates the possibility of milk allergy, one cause of the fussy and colicky baby. Because breast milk is a living substance and contains the enzyme lactase, which helps babies digest lactose, intolerance to lactose is rarely a problem. Although some babies may be allergic to substances in mother's diet that come through her milk, with a bit of detective work these can be detected and eliminated (see Key 15 for foods that may produce colic). High-need babies need frequent pacifiers; breastfeeding mothers find that they are their baby's pacifier, and much better than an artificial one. The term pacifier means "peacemaker"— how much more effective is mother than an artificial nipple!

The real payoff of breastfeeding is for mothers of fussy babies. A mother may be tempted to consider breastfeeding a high-need baby too draining or too demanding, forgetting what breastfeeding actually does for her. Although the mother of a fussy baby is constantly giving, giving, giving, the baby "gives" back to her a hormone, prolactin. This is a "perseverance hormone" that gives mother an added boost during those trying times. Many mothers report that breastfeeding has a calming effect on themselves as well as their babies—probably also due to prolactin. The act of breastfeeding forces mother to relax; it encourages her to put aside other seemingly more pressing obligations and tune into her baby. Prolactin is also called a "sensitivity hormone." Frequent breastfeeding stimulates a higher level of this hormone which, theoretically, should yield a higher level of maternal sensitivity.

Breastfeeding is especially helpful in inducing sleep for the restless baby and tense mother. Here is where the mutual giving really pays off. Recently a sleep-inducing protein was identified in mother's milk; when a baby suckles the mother receives an "injection" of the tranquilizing hormone prolactin. Thus mommy puts the baby to sleep and the baby helps put mommy to sleep. This is especially helpful in mothers who have a busy job outside the home and who are also blessed with a high-need baby. Upon returning home from work they find the relaxing effect of breastfeeding helpful for both of them.

Breastfeeding helps babies sleep. Besides mother's milk containing a natural sleep-inducing substance, researchers have found that frequent suckling of high-need breastfeeding babies has an organizing effect on the baby's sleep pattern. Breastfeeding helps mothers and babies sleep better. I have noticed how beautifully our infants drift off to sleep and how they radiate a feeling of contentment during and following breastfeeding. They seem to fade out immediately after breastfeeding, as if they had been given a shot of sleeping medication. Breastfeeding also helps mothers sleep. Mothers in my practice tell me that when they have trouble sleeping, they lie down and nurse their baby. This is again probably due to the relaxing effect of prolactin.

Marathoning. "She wants to nurse all night" is a common breastfeeding pattern for high-need babies, and sometimes all babies. There are several reasons for marathon nursing. In the first few months (usually around three weeks, six weeks, and three months), babies undergo several growth spurts, causing them to nurse frequently all day and night. This builds up the milk supply in response to baby's increasing nutritional needs. Another reason for marathon nursing at night is that around the second or third month babies become more sensitive to visual stimuli. During the day, these very aware babies are distracted by all the visual delights of their newly discovered world; we call them Mr. Suck-a-Little-Look-a-Little. They suck for a few seconds, look around, suck again, and are distracted again. At night, however, baby's world is not as visually stimulating. He is not as distracted (neither is mother), and he settles down to catch up on his meals. Mother may feel like an all-night diner, but if your tolerance level permits, I advise you to keep the diner open because baby is doing what he has to do. If your fatigue is becoming overwhelming, try these tips to minimize visual distractions during the day; nurse in a darkened and uninteresting room, a trick called "sheltered nursing." During feeding, remove siblings who are clamoring for attention and disturbing the little nurser.

According to recent studies, breastfed infants do awaken more often. This could be because breast milk is more rapidly absorbed, leaving the baby feeling less full than he would with formula. I suspect that mother's responsiveness to the waking and crying baby is a more important reason for the breastfeeding baby's waking more often. In general, breastfeeding mothers show a less restrained response to their baby's crying and find it more difficult to follow the "let them cry it out" advice. These mothers have built up such sensitivity to their babies that restrained nighttime parenting bothers them too much.

Formula-feeding the restless baby. As with breast-feeding, smaller, more frequent feedings tend to better satisfy these babies. Researchers feel that frequent feeding in general, whether by breast or bottle, has an organizing and calming effect on babies. If you suspect formula allergy, choose a hypoallergenic formula (see Key 10).

Filler foods. One of the longstanding remedies for prolonging sleep in infants is, "Fill baby up with cereal before bedtime." In fact, studies have shown that this makes no difference in the length of sustained sleep or the frequency of night waking. Some parents report that cereal before bed at around six months of age does help their baby sleep. It may be worth a try.

Nighttime bottles may be tried to induce sleep as part of the bedtime ritual or during the middle of the night. However, a baby should not be allowed to continue nursing from a bottle after falling asleep. When a baby falls asleep, he secretes less saliva and its rinsing action is less effective. This allows the sugars from the formula (or juice) to bathe the teeth during the night, resulting in severe decay of the front teeth—a condition known as bottle-mouth caries. What about the baby who just won't part with his nighttime bottle of milk or juice even after he has a lot of teeth? Some babies need to suck to sleep, even well into the second or third year. A useful trick that reflects this nighttime need yet prevents bottle-mouth dental caries is called "watering down." Each night very gradually dilute the juice or milk with water until after a few weeks the bottle contains all or almost áll water.

Above all, avoid the temptation to prop a bottle. Sometimes when baby has been feeding for a long time and you are tired, it's tempting to simply allow baby to lie in his crib sucking on a propped-up bottle. This is an unwise feeding habit for several reasons. If baby chokes, there is no one there to help him; and it deprives baby and mother of the social interaction of the feeding relationship. There should always be a person at both ends of the bottle.

Foods that interfere with sleep. There are several foods that can contribute to a fussy baby's already restless nature. Caffeine bothers some babies a great deal and some very little. It does pass through the milk of a breastfeeding mother and may disturb the sleep and behavior of the baby, but there is marked variability in how babies react to caffeine in mother's milk. For practical purposes a breastfeeding mother would have to ingest a lot of caffeine to affect her baby, but this isn't hard to do if she consumes such caffeine-containing foods as colas, tea, coffee and chocolate. Over-the-counter drugs such as cold and headache remedies and diet pills contain significant amounts of caffeine.

Nicotine may also have detrimental effects on restless babies. Smokers usually take longer to fall asleep and are awake more during the night, an effect similar to that of caffeine. Recent studies have shown that smoking may suppress prolactin levels in breastfeeding mothers. Mothers of high-need babies need all the prolactin they can get.

Alcohol in small amounts usually has no affect on the baby. It is false to believe that alcohol helps sleep. It may help a person get off to sleep sooner but often causes more restless sleep during the second half of the night and may cause the sleeper to wake up earlier. In general, excessive alcohol disturbs rather than improves sleep.

71

Junk foods, those high in cane sugar and artificial coloring, may interfere with sleep. Some infants are more vulnerable to the effects of junk foods than others. The cause of this is the effect of sugar on the insulin cycle, which results in blood-sugar swings and accompanying mood swings during the day and night. The best kinds of sugar for children are the natural sugars in dairy products, vegetables and fruit. Fructose sugars do not cause ups and downs in blood sugar and concomitant mood swings.

Foods that improve sleep are those containing the natural sleep inducer L-tryptophan—cheese, milk, eggs, pork, and veal. Suggested bedtime snacks are a glass of warm milk, cheese and crackers, a bowl of cereal with fruit, yogurt with fruit, and naturally sweetened ice cream.

16

~~~~~~

AVOIDING BURNOUT

B urnout is defined in one dictionary as "To stop burning from lack of fuel." Applied to parenting, burnout occurs when the demands exceed an individual's available energy. That parent can no longer adequately function within his or her profession. Mothers of restless babies often share with me, "I can't cope anymore." "I'm not enjoying motherhood." And the most despairing of all, "I can't cope, but I have to." Mothers, please bear in mind that burnout is not a sign of your inadequacies as a mother. In my experience burnout occurs more frequently in the best of mothers, those super-committed mothers, blessed with a demanding, restless baby. You have to be on fire before you can burn out.

Causes of burnout. A common cause of burnout is the supermom myth. Never before have mothers been required or expected to do so much for so many with so little support. In those critical few months after birth, many mothers are not permitted the luxury of just being a mother. Maternity leave should mean leave from all other obligations. In many cultures throughout the world the postpartum mother is given a servant, or *doula*, who takes over all the energy-draining household and social chores to free up the mother to divert her energy only to her baby. In our culture many mothers are expected to resume their previous roles as loving and giving wives, gourmet cooks, keepers of immaculate houses, gracious hostesses and contributors to the family income. The baby, meanwhile, is expected to fit conveniently into this lifestyle. This busy life and motherhood are often incompatible, even with modern labor-saving devices.

Another cause of burnout is the aloneness that many of today's mothers experience. There is no extended family to turn to for immediate advice and help, and many mothers have entered motherhood with inadequate role models. In most cultures the model of early motherhood is *babies* and *mothers* together. Today mother is alone. All of those convenient appliances make poor company, and they have nothing to teach a new mother about babies or about parenting. I believe that most new mothers are highly committed toward being a good mother and practicing the attachment style of parenting. Admittedly this style of parenting is the most exhausting, but it is not the style of parenting that causes mother burnout—it is practicing it in an unsupportive environment.

The temperament of the baby can contribute to mother burnout, but this should not be the case. It is true that mothers of high-need and restless babies are more prone to burnout, but when I delve into the family situation, I have rarely seen a case of burnout that can be attributed solely to the baby. If you look into each situation carefully there is usually some other factor that drains away the mother's energy, diverting it from what she should be doing (or wants to be doing) to what she is required to be doing (or thinks she is required to be doing).

Mother's stress test. The following factors predispose mothers (and fathers) to burnout.

- Ambivalent feelings during your pregnancy, especially about how the baby will interfere with your current lifestyle.
- A high-recognition career before becoming a mother.
- A history of difficulty in dealing with stress and of depression as a reaction to major changes.

- Poor prenatal preparation and unrealistic expectations of what babies are like.
- A stressful labor and delivery that did not go according to expectation.
- Medical problems at birth that separated mother and baby.
- A mismatch of temperaments between mother and baby (see Key 27).
- Marital discord and the expectation that the child will solve the problems.
- A highly motivated and compulsive mother.
- A mother committed to too many outside activities.
- A busy nest, a move or extensive remodeling or redecorating.
- Financial pressures.
- Illness in mother, father or baby.
- Successive babies who are less than two years apart.
- Family discord or problems with the older children.
- An uninvolved father—perhaps the most common cause.

Maternal burnout usually occurs when many of these risk factors are present, and it often carries over into the marriage. A burned-out mother can become a burned-out wife.

Recognizing red flags. Recognize the early warning signs of burnout. One of these is the feeling of not enjoying your baby. This indicates that you and your baby are not in harmony with each other. Another red flag is the feeling, "I am not a good mother." While occasional feelings of shaky confidence are normal, if these feelings of inadequacy persist and increase, seek help. Other signs are insomnia, making mountains out of molehills, forgetfulness, and lack of interest in personal hygiene and grooming. Dads, take note. In my experience of 20 years as a pediatrician and 25 years of marriage and fathering seven children, I have picked up one flaw in the otherwise perfect state of mother's intuition: mothers will continue to give, give, give until they are giving out before they either recognize it or seek help for it.

Survival tips.

1. **Prepare yourself during pregnancy for what babies are really like.** Many new parents do not realize how time-consuming a new baby actually is; a tiny baby can completely change a previously predictable, organized lifestyle. "Nobody told me it would be this way" is a common statement from mothers who had unrealistic expectations of the mothering profession. Pregnant mothers are so ecstatic at the aspect of having a baby that they usually tune out any thought that they may burn out.

2. **Get dad involved early.** In my experience one of the most common contributors of mother burnout is father walkout. Just as mothers are not noted for their ability to recognize the signs of impending burnout, fathers are also not known for their sensitivity to their wives' distress signals. As one mother told me, "I'd have to hit my husband over the head before he'd realize I'm giving out!" Don't expect your wife to ask for help. Be sensitive enough to anticipate what she needs: take over the care of the baby, do the dishes, hire household help. If you think your wife really would like some time off to herself to go shopping or have a massage but she feels she just can't get away, insist that she take the time, make the appointment for her, and drive her there.

3. **Know your limits.** Mothers vary greatly in their ability to cope with the high-need baby. Some mothers tolerate stress better than others. Some

76

are frazzled by one crying baby, while others are not ruffled by several babies and children crawling all over them. It is important to be honest with yourself and accept your coping abilities for what they are. If you have a high-need baby and you do not have a high level of tolerance for fussing, recognize this and use all these survival tips. In fact, child spacing would be advisable. During my years as a pediatrician and father I have been amazed at how many mothers cope so well (at least on the surface) with the many stresses of childrearing and family life. But I have also observed that many women do not know and accept their own limits. This is especially true of highly motivated mothers who want to be the "perfect mother."

4. **Practice the attachment style of parenting.** Attachment parenting helps you get in harmony with your baby, widens your acceptance level, makes your expectations more realistic, and generally increases your confidence.

5. **Define priorities.** Sit down and make a list of those daily activities that drain your energy away from your baby. With the support of your husband, scratch as many of these activities off the list as possible. For example, an exhausted mother in my practice recently told me she was a compulsive housekeeper until one day she looked at the kitchen floor and realized, "That floor doesn't have feelings. No one's life is going to be affected if that floor doesn't get scrubbed every day. My baby is a baby for a very short time, and she has feelings." This is part of maturing as a mother. You have to realize that if

ten things need to be done and you only have energy for eight of them, you should do only eight things. Just be sure to include all the ones with feelings.

6. **Do something for yourself.** Realistically, babies are takers and mothers are givers, and babies will continue to take until their own needs are completely filled. Babies are designed this way so that they can grow up to be loving, giving adults. But a mother cannot give continuously without being recharged periodically herself. It is often necessary for a husband, a friend, or a trusted health care professional to step in and *release* the mother for a bit of time off. Mothers often confide, "I just needed someone to give me permission to take some time for me. I felt like my baby needed me constantly." This is not meant to encourage a mother to become selfish or uncaring about her baby but rather to help her develop staying power in order that she can continue to mother in the way the baby was designed to be mothered. A very intuitive, organized mother who was coping well with the demands of her high-need baby put it this way, "I feel that even after birth my labor never really stopped and that I am still pregnant with a two-year-old. My life is a circle that revolves around her. What I need is a square that encloses her circle but leaves some corners just for me."

17

WHY BABIES SLEEP DIFFERENTLY THAN ADULTS

Babies' unique sleep patterns. Just as there are wide variations in babies' personalities, there are wide variations in their sleep patterns. It is important to approach parenting with no expectations, no preconceived images about what a baby should be like, especially how he should sleep. One tired mother shared with me, "Before our baby came, I thought that all newborn babies did was eat and sleep. All my baby did was eat." Babies' sleep patterns differ from those of adults. Most babies don't sleep through the night; they get their days and nights mixed up. They awaken frequently for feeding. One of the first things you will realize about nighttime parenting is that babies do what they do because they are designed that way. Here are some facts to help you understand how babies sleep differently than adults.

There are many stages of sleep, from very light to a very deep. For simplicity let's divide sleep into two stages: 1. light sleep (also called REM or rapid eye movement sleep) and 2. deep sleep (also called non-REM sleep). If you watch your baby sleeping you can easily identify which state of sleep she is in. In a state of light sleep, which is more active, the baby is squirming, her breathing movements are somewhat irregular, and sometimes her eyes are only partially closed. If you lifted her eyelids, you would notice that her eyeballs were often moving. This is why this state of light sleep is called REM or rapid eye movement sleep. When the baby is in the state of deep sleep, her body is much quieter, her respirations are regular, her limbs are dangling limp at her side and she is not easily aroused.

The times that babies and adults spend in these stages of sleep differ greatly. Adults spend only 20 to 25% of the total sleep time in REM sleep and the rest in quiet or deep sleep. The reverse is true for the baby, who as a newborn may spend as much as 80% of her sleep time in the state of REM sleep. The relative percentage of light sleep gradually decreases, so that by around three years of age a baby's sleep stages are more like those of adults—i.e., mostly deep sleep.

Babies have shorter sleep cycles than adults. Both babies and adults spend the whole night going in and out of sleep cycles, each of which comprises both a light and a deep state of sleep. Adults have sleep cycles lasting an average of 90 minutes, so that a period of light sleep occurs an average of four times a night. The sleep cycle in infants is shorter, around 60 minutes, so that an infant experiences nearly twice as many light sleep cycles as an adult in the same period of time. The *vulnerable period*—the time when the sleeper is most easily awakened—occurs at the transition from deep into light sleep. Because there are more sleep cycles for an infant, there are more vulnerable periods in the night when she may awaken.

Babies enter sleep differently than adults. When adults fall asleep they go quickly into the state of deep sleep, without passing through a long initial period of REM sleep. Adults can "crash" rather easily. Infants, on the other hand, routinely enter sleep through an initial period of light sleep lasting around 20 minutes. They then enter a period of transitional sleep followed by deep sleep. If an arousal stimulus (such as a disturbing noise) occurs during this initial light sleep stage or even during the transitional stage, the baby will awaken easily because he has not yet reached the quiet sleep stage. This accounts for the difficult-to-settle baby or the baby who has to be "fully asleep" before he can be put down. As babies mature they can go from being awake directly into the state of quiet sleep without first passing through a long period of light sleep. They settle more quickly; they can be put down to go to sleep. The age of going directly from waking to deep sleep varies from baby to baby, but it is seldom under three months. The fact that tiny babies enter sleep via the light sleep stage suggest an important nighttime parenting tip: infants should be *parented* to sleep, not just put down to sleep. Because the infant is more easily aroused from light sleep, he needs to be gentled through the initial light sleep stage until he descends into a deep sleep. To expect to put an awake baby into a crib, pat him on the back, say night-night and turn out the lights is unrealistic.

"But doctor, when will he begin sleeping through the night?" Only everybody else's baby sleeps through the night. The age at which babies settle varies tremendously. "Settling" means getting off to sleep more easily and staying asleep— that is, sleeping through the night. In the first few months most babies sleep 14 to 18 hours per day without any respect for the difference between day and night. A baby's sleep pattern resembles his feeding patterns—small, frequent feedings and short, frequent naps. Most newborns seldom sleep more than three or four hours at a stretch without awakening for a feeding. By four months of age the total amount of sleep decreases very slightly, but the organization of sleep patterns improves. Babies are awake for longer stretches and their sleep times are longer and fewer. As their developing brains become capable of inhibiting arousal stimuli, the relative percentage of deep sleep gradually increases. By four months of age most babies have developed some respect for waking during the day and sleeping at night. Studies have shown that during the first six months most babies do not sleep longer than five hours at a stretch during the night. As babies get older they approach sleep maturity. The total hours of sleep gradually decrease, the amount of light sleep decreases, deep sleep increases and the sleep cycles lengthen.

Babies' sleep patterns have survival and developmental benefits. Why do babies have these unusual sleep patterns? One of the facts I have learned throughout many sleepless nights as a pediatrician and a father is that babies do what they do for a reason. Babies do not maliciously want to deprive parents of their sleep. The high percentage of light sleep and frequent vulnerable periods of night waking have survival benefits to the infant. In the first few months the infant's needs are highest but his ability to communicate those needs is lowest. Suppose babies had adult sleep patterns and enjoyed more deep sleep than light sleep. If they were cold or hungry they might not awaken. If their noses were plugged and their breathing compromised, they might not awaken. I believe that the baby's sleep pattern is "infantile" so that he can more easily communicate his survival needs.

Besides the survival benefit, the predominance of light sleep in tiny infants has developmental benefits. Researchers believe that a preponderance of light sleep is important for the development of baby's brain. During the period of light sleep the higher brain centers continue to function, and it is believed that this continuing functioning is necessary for rapid brain growth during the first year. I mentioned this developmental phenomenon to one tired mother of a frequent night waker. She listened thoughtfully and finally decided, "Well, in that case, my baby is going to be very smart." Toward the end of the first year, as your baby's brain becomes more capable of blocking arousal stimuli, both you and the baby will probably enjoy a brief period of uninterrupted night sleep. However, just as you think your baby has kicked the night-waking habit, he may begin waking up again. Some children go to sleep easily and stay asleep; some go to sleep with difficulty but stay asleep; some go to sleep easily but do not stay asleep; and some children want neither to go to sleep nor to stay asleep. Fear, separation anxieties, disturbing dreams and nightmares are the main stimuli for night waking of children from one to three years.

High-need babies sleep differently. "Why do high-need babies need more of everything but sleep?" One of the "for better or worse" aspects of nighttime parenting is that babies usually carry their daytime temperament into the night. Some studies have shown that so-called "easy babies" go to sleep more easily and stay asleep longer than difficult babies. In these studies babies with more sensitive temperaments sleep an average of two hours less at night and one hour less during the day. This is a paradox for tired parents. You would think that high-need babies would need more sleep; their parents do. One tired father put it this way: "When it comes to sleep, I am a high-need parent."

High-need babies carry their temperamental daytime personalities into the nighttime. Parents will often describe their special baby as "tiring but bright." This brightness is what keeps high-need babies awake. They seem to be constantly awake and aware. It's as if they were endowed with an internal light that is not easily turned off.

The stimulus barrier is different in the high-need baby. Babies have a barrier that enables them to filter out unpleasant stimuli. One of the ways that most babies block out environmental stimuli is by falling asleep. High-need babies have an immature stimulus barrier. Their sensory thresholds are lower; in other words, you do not have to bother them much in order to get a reaction. High-need babies have increased sensitivity and are constantly aware of their environment. They are always tuned into and processing the delights of the world around them. Their radar systems don't shut down easily. High-need babies also take longer to develop sleep maturity. They seem to have longer and more frequent periods of light sleep. Consequently they are restless and squirming during the large part of the night. Some high-need babies enjoy a more intense kind of deep sleep; they really seem "zonked" when they are in the deep sleep stage. But high-need babies also seem to have more of the vulnerable periods of waking up when they pass from one sleep stage to the other. These babies are more of a challenge to put to sleep and to keep asleep.

18

WHY INFANTS AWAKEN AT VARIOUS AGES AND STAGES

Birth to three months. Most infants awaken frequently at this age because they are designed to. Tiny babies have tiny tummies and are frequently hungry. They have a high percentage of light sleep and infants at this stage are generally disorganized in all of their bodily functions, especially sleep. This is also a stage in which parents are juggling various styles and sleeping arrangements, and there is often a change of feeding from breast to bottle, or a combination, or frequent formula changes.

From three to six months many babies give parents a temporary rest and begin to sleep five or six hours straight. This is a much quieter stage in that most babies and parents have settled down into a semi-predictable nap time and night-time routine. Feeding patterns are established, nap patterns are established and bedtime rituals have been learned by trial and error. Just as the family has settled in to enjoy a good night's sleep, the next night waking stage occurs.

Six to nine months. The previous "good sleeper" may begin to wake up more frequently at this stage for several reasons. Teething pain often accounts for frequent night waking in a baby between five and seven months who previously settled well. Although you may not actually feel or see your baby's teeth until six or eight months, teething discomfort may start as early as four months and is accompanined by profuse drooling. A wet bed sheet under his head and a drool rash on his cheeks and chin where he rubbed his face on the wet sheets are signs that your baby may be teething. Teething can continue to be a problem as additional teeth appear all the way through the two-year molars. To minimize the fever and pain associated with teething, give your baby a pain-relieving medication, such as acetaminophen, before bed. There are also developmental reasons why babies awaken at this stage. Expect night waking any time your baby passes a major milestone in motor development, such as sitting up by himself (between six and seven months) and going from sitting to crawling (seven to eight months). I believe it is because babies spend so much time during the day exercising these newly found abilities that they also want to practice at night. When they sit up they are wobbly, fall over and wake up. When they try to crawl they may bang into the crib side, with the same result.

Nine to twelve months may be another more restful period for sleeping in some babies and a time of night waking in others. Separation anxiety begins at this stage; babies begin to be more aware of themselves as separate from mother and may not be able to handle this feeling of separateness. I believe that separation anxiety is a normal developmental phenomenon. At the very stage when a baby has the motor abilities to crawl away from mother, his mind tells him not to. This separation anxiety is often manifested in frequent night waking, especially in babies who sleep separately from their parents; or in a baby who previously slept well but now wakes up to seek nighttime company. Illnesses, especially virus-producing fevers, often begin at this stage. It is common for a previously good sleeper to have a cold or fever and then become a restless sleeper for several weeks thereafter. Some babies have difficulty resettling into previously regulated sleep patterns.

Twelve to eighteen months. Another major developmental milestone awakens babies at this stage—going from crawling to walking. Baby pulls himself up on the side of the crib and practices walking; suddenly realizing that he is trapped in the crib, he awakens and protests. Changes of diet and changes in sleep patterns are also frequent at this stage— breast to bottle, formula to cow's milk and trials of solid foods of increasing varieties and textures. Changing foods and eating patterns may bring about a change in sleep patterns. Babies are more social at this stage; they're in play groups, day care, church nurseries. As children share social skills they also share germs and illnesses, which may cause night waking.

Eighteen months on. This stage begins night waking primarily for emotional reasons. The most common causes are nightmares from upsetting daytime events, scary television, videos and motion pictures, recent family upsets, changes in lifestyle, a move or a death in the family. Parents, take heart. There will come a time when infants and children sleep through the night.

19

SLEEPING WITH PARENTS

Several times a day I am asked, "Doctor, is it all right for the baby to sleep in our bed?" My answer is invariably, "Wherever all three of you (mother, father and baby) sleep best and whatever leaves all three of you feeling right is the best sleeping arrangement for your family." Our first three infants settled easily at night in their own cribs. Our fourth child, Hayden, our high-need baby, awakened frequently from day one. By around a month of age my wife was exhausted from getting up and down like a yo-yo all night long to comfort Hayden. Finally, out of desperation, she took Hayden into our bed. From that night on the family slept better. Of course, three years later Hayden was still in our bed, but she eventually did wean into her own. Our last three babies comfortably nestled in our bed during their early years and at this writing our one-year-old shares our bed.

The term "family bed" has been popular lately. I prefer not to use this term as it conjures up visions of a whole lot of children in one small bed and dad on the floor somewhere. This works in cultures that have wall-to-wall mattresses; it seldom works in cultures with beds. I prefer the term "sharing sleep," whereby an infant sleeps with his parents until the time that he can comfortably sleep on his own. Because of the positive experience of sharing sleep in our family, over the past ten years I have been recommending this beautiful arrangement to parents in my practice. It works for most parents most of the time. It does not work for all parents all the time. But one message I definitely want to give to new parents trying to arrive at a sleeping arrangement that works for them: yes, it is okay to have your baby in your bed!

It is interesting that sleep sharing is following the course of other attachment styles of parenting, such as breastfeeding. Years ago it was taboo to have your baby in your bed or at least to tell anybody about it. In fact, many parents did and still do have their babies in their beds but they just don't tell their doctor or their mother-in-law about it. There was the fear that baby would never leave their bed, the fear of spoiling, the fear of sexuality disturbances and heaven knows what— none with any scientific or cultural basis. Each year the percentage of families who welcome their infant into their bed at least during the first year is gradually increasing, just like the incidence of breastfeeding. Why? Because it works and it feels right.

Advantages of sharing sleep. First of all, babies sleep better. In Key 17 we discussed that babies have a vulnerable period for waking up as they pass from deep sleep into light sleep. Since they have these sleep-cycle changes every hour, babies are vulnerable to waking up as often as once every hour. Sleeping with a familiar, predictable person helps baby settle through this vulnerable period and resettle himself into the next stage of sleep before he is able to awaken fully. In the first year, babies do not have object permanency—that is, when something is out of sight it is out of mind. Most babies under a year do not have the ability to conceive of mother as existing somewhere else. When a baby awakens alone, his aloneness may keep him from resettling into the next stage of sleep without awakening with a stressful cry. Waking up to a familiar attachment person often smooths the transition from one state of sleep to the next and may keep him from waking fully or at least help him resettle into the next state of sleep without a great deal of separation anxiety. When I wake in the morning and gaze upon the contented face of our "sleeping beauty," I can tell when he is passing through this vulnerable period because he often reaches out and touches one of us. When he reaches his anticipated target, a sleep-grin appears and an "I'm okay" expression radiates from his face. His eyes remain closed, and he often does not fully awaken.

Mothers sleep better. Parents, you may surprised at discovering that not only does your baby sleep better when sharing sleep, but so do you. The reason for this may be summarized in one word—*harmony*. I have previously stressed the importance of achieving harmony with your child during the day. Sleeping with your baby allows this harmony to continue so that baby and mother get their sleep cycles in sync with each other. When this harmony is achieved, babies awaken their mothers during their mutual light-sleep cycles and sleep during their mutual deep sleep cycles. Mothers are awakened less often from a state of deep sleep, which is what leads to the feeling of not getting enough sleep. Being awakened from a deep sleep by a hungry, crying baby is what makes the concept of nighttime parenting unattractive and leads to exhausted mother, fathers, and babies.

Besides this style of nighttime parenting being a harmonious relationship it is also a "hormoneous" relationship. In earlier keys we discussed prolactin as the mothering hormone. Three situations make prolactin increase in your body: 1. sleeping; 2. breastfeeding; and 3. touching your baby. Sleeping with your baby allows all three of these situations to occur throughout the night. When your baby shares sleep with you, he touches you and nurses from you, which may stimulate the release of more prolactin. It is noteworthy that it is not nighttime that stimulates prolactin but the act of sleeping itself. This is why mothers are encouraged to take frequent naps and to sleep with their babies during the day also. Mothers who share sleep with their babies and have mastered this nighttime harmony often tell me that as time goes on they seem to need less sleep and feel more rested despite their babies' waking and nursing frequently during the night. Perhaps this is due to the increased prolactin stimulated by the frequent night nurser.

Breastfeeding is easier. When a baby and mother are in close proximity they can meet each other's needs without either one fully awakening. A mother who had achieved this nighttime nursing harmony with her baby shared the following story with me: "About 30 seconds before my baby wakes up for a feeding, my sleep seems to lighten and I almost wake up (she is entering her phase of light sleep). By being able to anticipate his feeding, I usually can start breastfeeding him just as he begins to squirm and reach for the nipple. Getting him to nurse immediately keeps him from fully waking up, and then we both drift back into a deep sleep right after nursing." What happens is that the baby probably nurses through the vulnerable period for awakening and then reenters the state of deep sleep. What might have happened if mother and baby had not been right within "nursing range"? The baby would wake up in another room and would have to cry loudly to signify his needs. By the time the mother reached him, both mother and baby would be wide awake and probably angry, and would have difficulty in settling back to sleep.

I feel that sleep sharing is even more necessary with today's busy lifestyles. As more and more mothers, of necessity, are separated from their babies during the day, perhaps it is necessary to be reunited at night. In counseling mothers who plan to go back to work within a few months of their baby's birth, I encourage them to consider sharing sleep with their baby. It gives baby and mother the closeness at night that they miss during the day. Babies sleeping close to or with the parents is part of the natural continuum from mother's womb to mother's breasts to parents' bed, and weaning from all three of these places of security should occur only when mother and baby are ready. Sleep researchers have even suggested that mothers' and babies' sleep and dream cycles and brainwave patterns are in unison when they sleep and nurse together. There are also exciting experiments showing that failure-to-thrive babies (babies who fail to gain weight properly) do better when they share sleep. For example, a child care book written in 1840, *Management of Infancy* by A. Combe (New York, Fowlers and Wells), stated that "There can scarcely be a doubt that at least during the first four weeks and during winter and early spring a child will thrive better if allowed to sleep beside its mother's side and cherished by her warmth than if placed in a separate bed." One of the most time-honored medical treatments for the baby who is slow to gain weight is the advice to take him to bed and nurse. Science is just beginning to confirm what intuitive mothers have known all along—something good happens when babies and mothers share sleep.

20

ALTERNATIVE
SLEEPING
ARRANGEMENTS

Remember our sleeping arrangement philosophy: wherever all three of you sleep the best is the best arrangement for you. In some instances sleeping with the parents does not work for the infant or the mother. Some infants are too sensitive to their mother's presence and wake up more frequently, and some mothers report they wake up more frequently when they sleep next to their baby. If this is the case, try the following alternatives:

The sidecar arrangement. Parents who choose not to have their baby in their bed but who still want to sleep nearby can use the sidecar arrangement. Remove one side rail from the crib and place the open side of the crib adjacent to your bed. Adjust the crib mattress level to the exact level of your mattress. Be sure there is no crevice between your mattress and baby's. This arrangement works well with those families who want to try the family bed but don't have a king-size bed, or if the baby is such a squirmer that he needs his own space. A sidecar arrangement allows baby and parents to be in close touching distance and maintain their sleeping space.

The extended bed. As your baby outgrows the sidecar arrangement (or is displaced by a newborn), the extended bed is your next step. There are several ways to do this. 1. Place a twin bed or a rollaway bed adjacent to your bed. 2.

Place a mattress, sleeping bag, or futon on the floor near your bed. This is especially reassuring to the older child who may periodically reenter his parents' room because of a nightmare or during times of stress (sickness, moving, school, etc.). 3. Install a wall-to-wall mattress. In many other countries, such as Japan, the bedroom is one large mattress.

Sleeping with siblings. Oftentimes a baby sleeps with the parents for the first year or two (or longer), then is weaned into a sibling's room, and then gradually moves into her own room. Studies have shown that children under three sleep better sharing a bedroom rather than sleeping alone. Parents often report that siblings who sleep together quarrel less.

A child's own room. By the age of three, most children desire private space for their personal belongings. A child's own room helps foster a sense of order (shelves, compartments for toys, pegs for hanging) and a sense of responsibility for caring for his belongings. When children go through the stage of wanting more privacy, most want their own rooms. Separate bedrooms are not important enough to require a family to overextend financially. Mother and father should not have to work longer hours and further separate themselves from their children in order to have separate bedrooms.

What about the child who wakes up in the night and wants to come into the parents' bedroom? Expect this. During the preschool years expect a frequent nighttime visitor. Place the child's sleeping bag at the foot of your bed, leave your door open, and set the following rules: "If you come into mommy and daddy's room, you have to be quiet as a mouse, and tiptoe quietly and crawl into your sleeping bag. If you wake us up, you will have to go back to your own room." This is assuming that there is no medical or pressing emotional reason for waking up mommy and daddy.

21

~~~~~~

BEDTIME RITUALS: CONDITIONING BABY TO SLEEP

Sleep is not a state you can force a child into; it must overtake the child. The parents' role is to create a sleep-inducing environment. While I do not believe in rigid schedules and regimented nighttime parenting, it is true that to a certain extent sleep habits in babies are a learned response and a certain amount of conditioning may be necessary to help some babies fall off to sleep. It is important that when babies are presented with certain cues, they know that sleep is expected of them. Bedtime rituals set the stage and convey the message that sleep is soon to follow.

Choosing a bedtime. Many children do need predictable bedtimes and nap times. Some parents have a rigid and often unrealistic definition of bedtime: "Thou shalt go to bed at seven o'clock." At the other extreme are parents who define bedtime as whenever the child falls asleep. Because of changing lifestyles and family situations, rigidly early bedtimes are not as common and realistic as they used to be. The reason for this is that busy parents, especially fathers, often do not get home until six or seven o'clock. This is prime time for a baby and he is not likely to go right to sleep as soon as daddy gets home. There seem to be two reasons why parents are eager for early bedtimes: mother is worn out by the end of the day, and father does not enjoy spending an evening with a cranky baby. If mom or dad habitually gets home late in the evening, try the following: give your child a late afternoon nap so that he is well rested by the time father gets home. Baby and father can then enjoy this prime time together in the evening. In this situation, a later bedtime would be more practical. Babies will often learn to arrive at a sleep-wake schedule that best fits their needs within the family situation. This was true in our family with our youngest daughter, Erin. In the morning the whole household was very busy, with the other four children getting up and out. Erin learned to sleep through this chaos and awaken around 9:30 A.M. The older children return home around 3:30, so Erin learned to take her nap from 3:30 to 5:30. The chaos settles around dinnertime when daddy comes home. By then Erin was awake and refreshed and ready to enjoy a full evening with her family. She then willingly falls asleep around 10:00, or sometimes not until her mother and I go to bed. For most children, how they go to bed is more important than when they go to bed. If possible, be consistent in your bedtimes.

Suggested bedtime rituals:

- **Nursing down** (meaning comforting, not only breastfeeding). Nursing and a rocking chair are usually a winning combination for inducing sleep. Plan to be your newborn's moving bed. One of the telltale signs of a mother with a new baby is that she is always swaying back and forth a bit. She is simulating the motion the baby has been accustomed to during nine months in the womb.
- **A warm bath** before bedtime and a soothing massage will often relax both of you.
- **Swaddling.** Babies differ in how they like to be wrapped at bedtime. Some babies like to "sleep tight." Others like to "sleep loose." Some babies settle better in loose coverings that allow them more freedom of movement; others prefer to be securely swaddled in cotton sheets or baby

blankets. A mother once shared with me that she dressed her baby loosely during the day and swaddled him at night. This helped condition her baby to associate sleep with swaddling.

- **Cradles and other moving beds.** Some babies do not adapt well to being rocked to sleep in a rhythmic motion and then put down on a static bed; they need the bed to move awhile. Here is where the time-honored cradle comes in. As you put your baby down in the cradle, continue with gentle rocking at around 60 beats per minute, the heartbeat rhythm that your baby has grown accustomed to *in utero*. Instead of placing baby in the center of the crib or cradle, place him against you at one side; babies seem to like the security of sleeping against an object or person. This explains why they often squirm their way into a corner of the crib, against the side rail or against mommy or daddy in the family bed. If you don't have a cradle, putting little roller wheels on baby's bed and gently rolling it back and forth a few inches may lull baby to sleep.

- **Nestle nursing.** Your baby may be ready to fall asleep, but he just doesn't want to be put down alone. Rock and nurse him to sleep in your arms, either while walking or in a rocking chair. Then lie down with your sleeping baby on your bed and extend this time a bit longer until you are certain the baby is sound asleep (or until you are sound asleep). The smooth continuum from warm bath to warm arms to warm breast to warm bed will usually induce sleep.

- **Wearing down.** Many high-need babies associate being worn in the sling with rest or even sleep. When baby seems to be ready (or you are ready for baby to be ready for bed), put him in the baby sling and wear him around the house awhile until he drifts off to sleep in the sling. Then lie down on the bed and slip yourself out of the sling, leaving baby in it. This wearing down makes the transition from wakefulness to sleep much easier for the difficult-to-settle baby.

• **The laying on of hands.** Immediately after being put down to bed, some babies will squirm a bit and their heads will bob up and down, giving you the signal that they are not in deep enough sleep to be left alone. In this case, father (he has a bigger hand) can lay his hand on the back or head of the baby or put one hand on the head and one the back. The warmth of the secure hand may be the added touch that is needed to help baby give up his silent protest and drift off to sleep. Patting baby's back or bottom rhythmically at 60 beats per minute may add the finishing touches to the ritual of inducing sleep. Remove your hands gradually, first one, then the other, easing the pressure slowly so as not to startle baby back to waking. We have observed an interesting phenomenon in laying hands on our babies: you must be very gradual in removing your hand, even allowing it to hover above your baby's skin before removing it completely.

• **A warm fuzzy.** I learned this sleep-inducing technique while giving a talk at a parenting seminar in Australia. I looked out into the audience and noticed that many mothers who brought their babies also brought along a lambskin. After they rocked their babies to sleep they would lay them down on the lambskin; the babies had learned to associate the fur with sleep. Even though baby was in a strange place, the lambskin was his familiar "bed" and he slept better. These mats are specially shorn to be both safe and comfortable for babies, as well as machine washable. If your baby gets a stuffy nose from the lint, cover the lambskin with a sheet or cloth diaper.

Baby's sleeping positions. A newborn usually sleeps better on his stomach than on his back because his breathing is more effective while lying on the stomach. In the first few weeks, tiny infants are best placed on their sides to sleep; this is achieved by rolling up a towel and wedging it in the crevice between baby's back and the mattress. Theoretically, positioning baby on his right side is best as this allows the stomach to empty by gravity. After the first few weeks, babies will seldom remain on their sides very long but will roll over onto their stomachs. When placing a baby on his stomach, turn his head to one side. Don't worry about him suffocating. Even a newborn is able to lift his head off the mattress momentarily to turn it to one side.

What happens if none of these bedtime rituals works? As a last resort try:

Freeway fathering. Put your baby in a safe car seat and go for a ride; nonstop motion is best. Take a drive on the freeway to avoid the stops and starts of city driving, as this may awaken baby. When your baby has fallen into a deep sleep, return home and place the sleeping baby (still in the car seat) in the bedroom. When our 23-year-old son, Jim, and his wife were babysitting for our one-year-old, Stephen, he tried this technique. When we arrived home and found Stephen sleeping, we asked Jim how he had been able to get the baby to sleep. He proudly replied, "I used freeway fathering." I was overjoyed that Jim had picked up on my fathering techniques. Yes, dads, we do model fathering for the next generation.

22

KEEPING BABY ASLEEP

Now that you are an expert on bedtime rituals and putting your baby to sleep, let us explore ways of keeping her asleep.

Develop a sleeping arrangement that works. Some babies stay asleep better in their parents' bed, some in their own room, some in their own bed in their parent's room. The important thing is to be open to trying what works for your family. You may also find that no one arrangement works at all times for your baby.

Respond promptly to baby's awakening signal. The most vulnerable period for awakening is when baby ascends from a deep sleep into light sleep. Sometimes babies will whimper and squirm for a few seconds and resettle themselves without any outside help as they pass through this vulnerable period. Some babies are more adept at self-soothing than others. If your baby is not a self-soother and he is not promptly attended to, he will awaken completely, angrily, and you may be up for the rest of the night. When baby awakens during this vulnerable period, get to him quickly. Soothe him with nursing or a reassuring laying on of hands. If you parent your baby through this vulnerable period, you can prevent him from awakening completely. I have noticed that during this vulnerable period my own babies seemed to direct their radar systems toward mommy and moved in to nurse. The more easily available their target, the less they awaken.

Create a quiet environment for sleep. For most sleeping babies, you don't have to tiptoe around and create a noiseless environment. Our first baby was born while I was an intern and his bedroom was adjacent to my study. He slept right through music, study noises, telephone rings, and all the ambient sounds of student life. Other babies need a quiet environment. The most common arousal stimuli are startling noises, light, hunger, loneliness, and discomfort. You can create a calmer sleeping environment by lessening the stimuli:

- Provide a warm body to sleep with.

- Soundproof the sleeping area as much as possible. Oil the springs and joints of a squeaky crib. Get the barking dog out of earshot—before it barks. Take the phone off the hook.

- If your child has a pain-producing illness or discomfort, such as teething, check with your doctor about giving an appropriate dosage of acetaminophen.

- Use opaque shades to block out light.

- Make sure baby has a comfortably full tummy. A hungry baby or child will awaken, but a stomach that is too full will also interfere with sleep. Nursing before bedtime usually suffices for the young infant. Stuffing a baby full of cereal to get him to sleep through the night usually doesn't work, but may be worth a try if nothing else does. A glass of milk and a nutritious cookie, a bowl of cereal, or some fruit makes a good bedtime snack for the young child.

- Leave a little bit of mother behind. To keep your baby sleeping, especially if you have a separation-sensitive baby, leave a bit of yourself in the bed with her. One mother of a tiny baby noticed that her baby settled better when she left her nursing bra in the cradle.

- A continuous tape recording of you singing a bedtime song or lullaby may help.

Mother substitutes are becoming big business. You can buy a high-priced teddy bear with a tape recorder in his gut that sings a song or even has breathing sounds. Baby can then snuggle up to the breathing bear. As a concerned father, I do not want my babies going to sleep to the sound of anyone else's voice. Though this may be useful as an occasional parent substitute, why not use the real parent?

"Playing dead." Some infants and children waken in the middle of the night ready to play. Here is where conditioning is often necessary for sheer survival. We simply let our baby sit there between us while we continue sleeping (or pretending to sleep), ignoring her desire to play. You are conveying the non-negotiable message to your child that if she is in bed with you, she sleeps when you sleep and does not play. Beds are for sleeping in, not for playing in. Again, a bit of humor is necessary for nighttime survival.

Delaying the early riser. The child who pops into your bedroom and wants to play can be a trial to tired parents. Purists may claim that a baby should be allowed to follow his own biorhythms for awakening at dawn. It is easy to say this about someone else's baby. But babies can be fooled as to what time it really is. Oftentimes a slight bit of light coming through the window at dawn is just enough to awaken a baby, especially if that ray of light happens to strike during a period in her sleep cycle when she is vulnerable to being awakened. The following suggestions may prolong sleep in your early riser:
- Dark, opaque curtains or shades may prolong the nighttime environment.
- Lay down rules for noiseless wakening with the early riser's older siblings.
- Give the child an alarm clock "just like daddy's." When the alarm goes off, the child may get up, just like daddy does.

- Leave a box of things to do beside your child's bed in order to entice him to stay in his room and play quietly by himself for awhile.

- Leave a nutritious snack on a bedside table to tide the hungry riser over until breakfast.

Bedtime rituals and stories for older infants and children. Tired fathers will often lament, "It takes me two hours to put her to bed." Children are clever nighttime procrastinators, but if you consider this habit from the child's standpoint, it's reasonable. Dad has been away from them all day long and now they are going to try to prolong this prime time with him as long as possible. There are nights when you know your child is tired but she just won't give up and go to bed. The problem is not that she doesn't want to go to bed; it is that she doesn't want to be separated from you or to give up the delights of the day. Older infants and children also need a "winding down" activity, such as a warm bath, a soothing story, a back rub, gradually dimming lights (a dimmer switch in a child's bedroom is a wise investment), and bedtime prayers. Lying down with your child and mothering or fathering him to sleep can often alleviate the separation sensitivity that is really the main reason why children don't want to give up and fall asleep. Avoid exciting and stimulating activity such as wrestling at bedtime. This will only serve to wind up the child rather than wind him down. The following bedtime tips were given to me by creative parents of older children:

- Massage game. "Keep your eyes closed, don't peek, what am I rubbing now?"

- Back rub game. "Plant a garden" on your child's back using different touches for different foods, which your child selects. Gradually lighten your strokes as you smooth out the garden.

- An alarm clock buzzer to signal "bedtime in five minutes."

103

To avoid a conflict of wills, let the clock announce the bedtime.

- A game of "whoever's in bed first picks the story."
- Use an egg timer. "When all the sand hits the bottom, the lights must go out." Your child may get tired watching the sand fall.

Bedtime stories are a wonderful way to spend some quality time with your child and also to get her to sleep. Bedtime is also a good time to teach moral and ethical lessons to a child. Children love homemade stories. Choose some moral lessons that you want to teach (such as, it is wrong to steal or lie) and fabricate a story to teach this lesson. Bedtime is a prime time of receptivity for children to listen to a story without feeling that they are being preached to. Children also love stories about when their parents were children; these help them understand about your own childhood. Choose a book that you enjoy too, so when your little one asks the inevitable "read it again," you won't mind complying. Avoid stories with gremlins, monsters, and ghosts, as they are more likely to keep your child awake than induce sleep. In fact, for a sleepless child it is wise to avoid scary television and books during the day as well. Children tend to exaggerate images in their dreams; a harmless-seeming cartoon may become a scary image in a dream.

The best sleep-inducing type of story that has worked in our family is one that involves counting. I'll ask our three-year-old, Matthew, what type of story he would like me to tell. He may ask for one about Batman and Robin. My story would be, "Batman and Robin went fishing ... and they caught one fish, two fish, three fish, four fish, etc., etc., etc." Sometimes it would take 50 fish to put him to sleep, sometimes 25. Counting stories nearly always work. Soften your voice and slow down your speed toward the end of the story. This little trick helps children fade out sooner.

23

SOUNDS THAT SOOTHE

Sounds of the womb. Sounds that calm the fussy baby and settle the restless baby are those that most closely resemble the rhythm and sounds of the womb. These include:

• Records of mothers' heartbeats and other recordings of womb sounds
• Running water from a water or shower
• Tape recordings of ocean waves, waterfalls, rainfall
• A bubbling fish tank
• A loudly ticking clock
• A metronome

White noise. Sounds that involve all the frequencies audible to the human ear and are continuous and monotonous are very effective in settling the restless baby and keeping her asleep. The noise is repetitive and without meaning and lulls the mind into oblivion. Such noises can be produced by:

• A fan or air conditioner
• A dishwasher
• A vacuum cleaner

Continuous-play tape recordings are effective—mother or father singing lullabies is perfect. The lower, more monotonous, and more rhythmical the tone, the more soothing. Tape recordings of baby's own cry played during a crying episode can surprise her into silence, giving you a chance to apply other comforting measures. Use a tape recorder that has continuous playback. One mother I know went through several vacuum cleaners before she realized that she could accomplish the same result by tape recording the vacuum cleaner sound. Sound ridiculous? Not really. If you have ever had a fussy baby, you will try anything that works.

Music to sleep by. Babies settle best with classical music rather than turbulent rock music. Choose music that is simple and consistent, such as flute and classical guitar. Studies have shown that even babies in utero are calmed by the music of Mozart and Vivaldi but excited by rock. Select your own sleep-inducing medley. Select pieces that are proven to soothe your baby and prepare a continuous tape from recordings of these pieces. The following selections have been suggested to me by parents of fussy babies:

• *Third Brandeburg Concerto* by J. S. Bach
• Harp music by Boildieu
• *Lullaby* by Brahms
• *Clair de Lune, Dances Sacred and Profane, Piano Preludes, and Prelude to Afternoon of a Faun* by Debussy
• *Serenade for Strings* by Dvorak
• String quartets by Haydn
• *Symphony #17 in G Major*, first movement, by Mozart
• Piano works by Ravel
• Indian flute music played by Jean-Pierre Rampal
• Indian music and Bengali chants.
• Selections available from local infant massage instructors
Above all, select music that both you and your baby enjoy.

24

~~~~~~

HELPING THE HIGH-NEED BABY TO SLEEP BETTER

High-need babies are usually restless sleepers, mainly because they carry their bright temperament into the nighttime, they have immature stimulus barriers to block out arousal stimuli, and they may have special sleep cycles with more vulnerable periods to awaken. Here are some sleep survival tips:

1. **Nursing down.** It is totally unrealistic for the parents of a high-need baby to put him down in a crib and expect to watch him settle himself into a deep slumber. It seldom works that way. These babies need to be parented to sleep rather than just put to sleep. They need help shutting down. A technique that has been successful in our family is what we call "nursing down": put your baby in a baby sling and walk with him until he is in a state of deep sleep (this usually takes between 20 and 30 minutes). You will recognize the state of deep sleep by the "limp limb sign," with baby's arms dangling weightlessly from his sides. Bend over the bed and slip the sling over your shoulder with baby still in the sling; place him on the bed, using the sling as a cover. If you try to put the high-need baby down to bed before he is in a state of deep sleep, he will very likely

wake up and demand that you repeat the whole bedtime ritual. In fact, it will probably take longer the second time around. These babies are so ultrasensitive that a change in position or the change in gravity that comes with going from your arms down to the bed is enough to awaken them from light sleep.

2. **Nestle nursing.** If the nursing down technique does not work (I use nursing here to mean comforting, not only breastfeeding), then try nestle nursing. Curl up next to your baby and nurse her off to sleep. These bright little babies do not seem to want to make the transition from waking to sleeping alone and need to fall asleep accompanied by somebody. Also take advantage of the sleep-inducing effects of breastfeeding as mentioned in Key 15.

3. **Share sleep with your baby.** While sharing sleep may be beneficial for most babies, it is almost a must for high-need babies; to most high-need babies, "crib" is a four-letter word. It is the nature of these sensitive babies to want harmony in their environment both by day and by night. When mother and baby are close to each other and baby begins to stir and enter a vulnerable period of night waking, mother can simply nurse the baby right through it and help him enter the state of deep sleep. Mother's deep sleep is not interrupted, and she feels more rested.

4. **Start the next day off right.** Ever hear the old saying, "He got up on the wrong side of the bed"? Well, he probably went down on the wrong side of the bed. Parenting a child to sleep, instead of simply putting him to bed, has a mellowing effect

on his daytime behavior. The state of relaxation immediately before drifting off to sleep is called the alpha state. It is believed that thoughts occurring during the alpha state are most likely to be remembered and carried over into awakening in the morning. If an infant goes off to sleep at mother's breast or in father's arms he feels right. A child who goes to sleep feeling right is more likely to awake feeling right, and will begin the next day on a positive note—a real plus for the high-need baby and his parents.

Contrast the child who was put down in a crib and left to cry himself to sleep alone. He goes to bed angrily and is therefore likely to awaken in an angry mood. He certainly is destined to "get up on the wrong side of the bed." A little extra energy spent with your baby at the end of the day may save you a lot of wasted energy the next day.

25

MEDICAL CAUSES OF NIGHT WAKING

A sick child is likely to awaken at night. Many childhood illnesses seem to be worse at night. One of the reasons is that a child who is alone has nothing to distract him from his illness. Also, the fever that accompanies a virus tends to be higher at night and will wake a sleeping child. The following are common medical causes for night:

A stuffy nose may cause night waking. Because babies have narrow nasal passages and are nose- rather than mouth-breathers, the slightest amount of nasal congestion can bother and awaken them. If your baby has a stuffy nose at night, here is how to clear it. Prepare some nose drops with a pinch of salt and a glass of water (no more than ¼ teaspoon salt to 8 ounces water). With a plastic eye dropper, squirt a few drops into each nostril. These drops loosen the secretions and may stimulate your baby to cough or sneeze, which is his own protective mechanism for clearing his breathing passages. After a few minutes, take a rubber bulb syringe (a nasal aspirator, available at any drugstore) and gently suck out the loosened secretions. Most babies protest at this intrusion into their nose, but it is necessary. Using a humidifier or vaporizer in dry climates and during months of dry central heating will also help to keep your baby's nose clear. Babies usually settle much better when their breathing is easy.

Allergies. In addition to environmental irritants, allergies, especially to substances in the child's sleeping environment, can increase nasal and respiratory secretions and interfere with sleep. The most common respiratory allergens that affect your baby are dust, cow's milk products, perfumes and hair sprays, animal dander (keep pets out of the child's bedroom), plants, clothing (especially wool), stuffed animals, feather pillows, down comforters, blankets, and fuzzy toys that collect dust. Defuzz the crib and bedroom. Get all the stuffed animals, fuzzy toys, feather pillows, and other dust collectors and temporarily bury them in the garage.

Most infants' and children's bedrooms are one big allergy pit. Wash baby clothing and bedclothing before using them. If your child has a lot of nasal allergies, use washable throw rugs on the floor instead of shag or pile carpet, if possible. Dust blinds and drapes frequently. In severe cases a room air purifier is necessary. Above all, have a no-smoking rule around baby's room.

Telltale signs that your baby is allergic to something in his sleeping environment are a clear, runny discharge from his nose or eyes, sniffles, or persistent nasal congestion when he awakens. Eliminating potential allergens from your child's bed and bedroom will help him sleep better.

What about nighttime fever? If your child has had a fever during the day but it seems to be gone right before he goes to bed, it is still wise to give him a temperature-lowering medicine before going to bed. Most viral illnesses produce a higher fever at night than during the day. Fever is likely to awaken a child. It is usually unwise to awaken a sleeping child to give fever-lowering medications, unless advised to do so by your doctor. It is not necessary to awaken a sleeping child to take his temperature; just feel or kiss his forehead.

Ear infections are one of the most common medical causes of night waking in the infant and young child. Here is

111

"Dr. Bill's rule" for recognizing when a common cold has become an ear infection:

- When the discharge from the child's nose changes from clear and watery to thick and yellow (a runny nose becomes a snotty nose).
- When your child has a cold plus yellow drainage from his eyes.
- When your child's personality during a cold changes from happy to cranky.
- When his sleep patterns change from sleeping well to restlessness and increased night waking.

If your child's cold has progressed to an ear infection, he needs medical attention.

Unfortunately, ear infections seem to bother a child more at night. When a child is lying down, the fluid from the infection presses on the eardrum. When he sits upright, the fluid drains away from the eardrum and there is less pressure. This is why infants with ear infections sit or stand up in their cribs at night, and mothers relate that they seem better when held. A child with an ear infection may awaken frequently during the night but seem better during the day. Don't interpret this as a sign that the infection is improving; take the child to the doctor.

Sometimes the fluid accumulated behind the middle ear builds up and the resulting pressure creates a rupture through the eardrum, causing drainage out the infected ear. If you see drainage resembling thick mucus around the opening of the ear canal or on the child's pillow near his ear, seek medical attention even though the child's pain is gone. When an eardrum ruptures, the pressure is released and therefore the pain is relieved; this gives a false sense of security that the child is "better." Chronic low-grade ear infections are a medical cause of chronically restless and cranky children. There is what I call an "ear personality"—an infant or child who has a persistent cold and who undergoes a personality change from previously happy to cranky, irritable, restless, and "a bear to live with." If your infant or child has these signs, have his ears checked.

A nighttime parenting tip for ear infections: if your child awakens with a sore ear at night, it is seldom necessary to call your doctor since antibiotics take around 12 hours to work anyway. To alleviate the pain and get your child through the night, try the following self-help remedies:
- Try to get your child to sleep propped up at a 30-degree angle on a couple of pillows. This takes the pressure off the eardrum.
- Give your child a double dose of acetaminophen; this can be repeated in three to four hours.
- Squirt three or four drops of warm vegetable oil into your child's ear and put an oil-moistened cotton ball gently in the ear canal to keep the oil in. Let your child sleep with the painful ear up, allowing the warm oil to soothe the inflamed eardrum. Sometimes a story will also help to soothe the hurting child back to sleep.

Pin worms look like tiny pieces of white thread about one-third inch long. The pregnant female pinworm travels down the intestines and out the rectum to lay her eggs, usually at night. This activity results in intense itching, which often causes the child to awaken and scratch the egg-infested area around his anus and buttocks. These eggs are picked up under the fingernails and transmitted to the child's mouth, to other children or to other members of the household. The swallowed eggs then hatch in the intestines, mature, reproduce, and repeat the lifecycle.

Frequent night waking with itching symptoms and scratch marks around your child's anus suggest that he may have pinworms. Sometimes the tiny worms can be seen at night in the dark if you spread your child's buttocks and shine a flashlight on the anus. Little girls may have pinworms near the vagina, causing a vaginal itch. If you cannot see the worms but you still suspect they're there, place a piece of adhesive tape sticky side out on a popsicle stick or tongue depressor and press it against the anus to capture the eggs. The tape test is best performed as soon as your child awakens, before his bath or bowel movement. Take the tape to the doctor, where it can be examined under a microscope for pinworm eggs and treatment can be prescribed.

A nighttime pain tip: Many young children, and even older ones, have periodic abdominal pains and headaches which have no identifiable medical cause, do not harm the child, and subside without treatment. As a general rule, pain that awakens the child at night is of greater concern than pain occurring during the day. This is especially true with abdominal pain and headaches. If these begin to awaken the child at night, seek medical attention.

26

BABYSITTING THE
FUSSY BABY

Because of the oneness that develops between a high-need baby and its mother, the pair may seem inseparable for the first year or two. Babies do not want to separate from the mother or mother from babies. It is important for the new mother of a high-need baby not to feel isolated or to feel that she must stay home all the time. "Home" to a tiny baby is where the mother is, and you can get used to wearing your baby in many places. But there are times when you and/or your husband will feel the need to get away. High-need babies are not noted for their acceptance of substitute caregiving, which may even increase your guilt of leaving your baby. Here are some ways to manage substitute caregiving.

Choose a caregiver who sincerely mirrors your own parenting style—a sensitive person who is genuinely bothered by a baby's cry. If you are uncertain of the caregiver's sensitivity level, tell her how you want your baby mothered in your absence: when he cries he should be picked up and comforted. Ask her how she will do this. As a sensitivity test you may even ask, "What will you do when my baby cries?"

Passing the baby. We have used a technique we call "pass the baby" to comfortably make the transition from ourselves to our babysitter. Our high-need baby loves to be carried in the baby sling and will usually drift off to sleep in the evening when we carry him. When we are ready to go out, we pass the baby to the babysitter while he is still in the sling and he will often stay calm or even asleep. Making a smooth transition from one baby-wearer to another can increase the baby's acceptance of the substitute caregiver and make substitute parenting easier for the babysitter. Transitioning in a baby sling is particularly useful for babies who have trouble falling asleep for anyone but the mother. Wear baby until he falls asleep in the sling, then lie down on the bed and slip yourself out of the sling using the carrier as a cover. Since baby is used to this style of going to bed for the parents, he is more likely to accept it from the babysitter.

One of the inevitable questions parents ask is, "When can we leave our baby for a few nights?" Being able to leave your baby depends upon three variables: your need to get away, your baby's sensitivity to separation, and the effectiveness of the substitute caregiver. In general I advise parents to travel as a threesome at least for the first couple of years. If there are occasions in which you want to or must be away from your baby for a few days, consider these suggestions for nighttime parenting:

- Try to make as few changes as possible in baby's routines. Be sure you leave detailed instructions with the substitute caregiver about how you want your baby mothered during the day and at night.
- If your baby is used to sleeping with you, then continue having him sleep with somebody.
- If your baby has naptime routines, be sure to leave instructions for the caregiver on how to mother the child to sleep.

27

NAPPING

Some babies seem not to need many naps, but all parents need their babies to take naps. Naps are usually necessary for babies and children to thrive and for mothers to survive.

How often does a baby need to nap? Napping has restorative value for both infants and parents. It helps recharge their energies to have a pleasant day and a better night. But there is wide variation in babies' nap requirements. Too many naps may cause baby to sleep poorly at night. Too few may result in a cranky baby during the day. The key is to identify just the proper number and duration of naps your baby needs at a given age to achieve daytime contentment and nighttime sleepiness. A newborn's napping pattern resembles his feeding scale—small, frequent feedings and short, frequent "catnaps." In the early months a baby may nap frequently and retreat into the comfort of sleep to shut out unpleasant stimuli. He may sleep as much during the day as at night. Around three months of age, most babies will begin to sleep more at night and have two nap periods during the day, one in the morning and one in the afternoon. For the remainder of the first year most babies will continue a pattern of a one-hour nap in the morning and a one- to two-hour nap in the afternoon. Between one and two years, most babies drop the morning nap but still require a one- to two-hour afternoon nap. Most toddlers need at least a one-hour afternoon nap up to the age of three or four.

Nap when your baby naps. I encourage a mother to nap when her baby does. It is a mistake to use baby's naptime to "finally get something done." You need the nap just as much as baby does. This is part of getting in harmony with your baby, in order that you both survive and thrive during those exhausting early months.

Observing naptime signs. Watch for cues that your baby needs a nap or at least some time out. If a baby was previously happy and playful but gradually begins to fuss or start overreacting to stimuli, he may need a little down time with quiet rocking—or he may need a nap. Sometimes a baby needs just a few minutes to quietly nestle and rock in mother's arms; he is then resettled and can contently resume play. Others will follow this brief time out with a full nap. Some babies give definite cues when they're ready for a nap: increasing crankiness, droopy eyelids, slowing down in activity, putting the head down on the floor, or wanting to cuddle or nurse. Some babies will not even wait for someone to read their nap cues. We have occasionally walked into a room and found our baby napping in unusual places—under the piano, on the couch, under a table, or sometimes right in the middle of the floor.

Enticing the reluctant napper. You can not force an infant to nap, but you can set the stage for a sleep-inducing environment that allows sleep to overtake the child: a dark, quiet place, relaxing music, or lying down with your child. Most infants do better with consistent naptimes. I encourage parents to choose a time of day when a nap is most convenient, or when they are the most tired. For a period of a week or two, lie down with your infant at those convenient times. Be as consistent as possible. Many infants and children need a predictable sequence of events to condition them to nap. This sequence may be lots of exercise, followed by lunch, followed by a story, followed by sleep-inducing music or a lullaby in a dark, quiet room. When a child gets used to these conditioning steps that lead to a nap, sleep usually follows. Conditioning is easier for the toddler and older child than in early infancy. If you have a reluctant napper, it may be necessary to nap with your child during this two-week conditioning period. In the beginning he may refuse to sleep; that is all right. Simply lie down with the child in a dark, quiet room, read him a story or turn on soft music, and nap yourself. After a few days the child will usually get the idea that this is his "time out." He may fully nap or at least doze a bit.

Parents with busy lifestyles may need to juggle their child's naps around their schedule. Babies can quite easily learn to nap on the run, in baby carriers and car seats. I remember when our eighteen-month-old daughter Erin became accustomed to napping in her car seat during the afternoon carpool time when Martha was picking up the older children at school.

Sling napping. This is particularly useful for the reluctant napper. Choose a time of day that is most enjoyable for you to take a relaxing walk, preferably outdoors in a park during mild weather. Try to make it around the time that you wish your child to nap. Put the baby in a sling and wear him for a long walk and nap. Babies who are used to being worn a lot in a carrier are often conditioned to nap as soon as they are placed in it and the caregiver begins walking. For new mothers who feel a bit housebound, this is a chance for some exercise while inducing a nap for your baby. Sling napping is particularly useful for newborns, for whom motion, not stillness, is a natural state.

Naptimes need to be flexible in today's busy lifestyles. Early risers are usually ready for an early morning

119

nap and an early afternoon nap. These are babies who are ready for bed at seven or eight o'clock in the evening. But late morning and late afternoon naps are perhaps in keeping with the busy lifestyles of most of today's households. If baby's afternoon nap is too early, he is often cranky in the late afternoon or early evening, just at the time when parents arrive home from work. At prime time it is no fun for tired parents to be greeted with a tired baby. A late afternoon nap (with resulting later bedtime) allows a baby to be more rested for prime time with parents in the evening.

Synchronizing naptimes. Synchronizing naptimes may be difficult when you have a new baby and a toddler. In juggling naptimes you may need to call in some reserves. While your newborn naps, you might get your two-and-a-half-year-old involved in a play group for a few afternoons each week. Sometimes mom and dad can do shift work; dad takes the older child and mom naps when the baby naps. Sometimes your tiny baby and toddler may be ready for some quiet time together. Before you put the baby down to nap, turn on some music and place the toddler in a quiet, safe play area with easy access to you should you be needed. Then lie down and nurse your baby off to sleep. This arrangement usually allows the mother to doze with the tiny baby while at the same time keeping one ear open for her resting toddler. If your toddler still demands your attention during your infant's naptime, place the infant in a baby sling and sit on a comfortable couch. Now you have two hands free to read a sleep-inducing story to the toddler during which time, hopefully, all three of you will drift off to sleep.

Where to nap? Anywhere you can. Many children resist naps because they don't want to be isolated in a room alone when there are so many fun things going on in the rest of the house. Some children will crash for a nap anywhere in the house. You can eliminate some naptime hassles by not insisting that the child nap in his own bedroom, although this may be preferable. For our occasional reluctant nappers, we fabricate a "nap nook"—a special place in a corner on a mat, a little tent made of blankets, or a large box with one side cut out, into which the child crawls when he is tired. This technique capitalizes on children's natural desire to construct their own little retreats in all the nooks and crannies throughout the yard and house. Lambskin mats are also a good place for babies to nap and a way to condition them to sleep. I have seen mothers take lambskin with them wherever they go.

Pleasant and consistent naptimes. Pleasant and consistent naptimes are a prelude to encouraging healthy sleep habits at night. A child who is a content napper is more likely to become a good nighttime sleeper.

28

NIGHT WAKING AND
WORKING MOTHERS

I f you return to full- or part-time work outside the home,
expect the baby to change his sleep habits. Picture the
following common scenario: mother, after work, picks up
her baby from the sitter, who exclaims, "My, what a good
baby; he slept all day!" This good baby by day becomes a
night waker; he has tuned out the babysitter during the day
and then starts waking up to get more attachment from mom
at night. Even six-month-olds seem to try to get the level of
attachment they need. They do not stop and think, "Mom is
tired from working all day, she needs her sleep at night, and
I think I will leave her alone."

Another common ploy for the older infant or child when
mother returns to work is to suddenly want to sleep in the
parents' bedroom. The previously contented sleeper suddenly
appears as a frequent nighttime visitor. The key to surviving
night waking is to be resilient in trying varying sleeping arrangements, just as you expect the child to be resilient in
adjusting to different caregiving arrangements. Working
mothers seem to be master jugglers, and nighttime juggling
is part of this change of lifestyle.

Here are some tips for surviving working and night waking with the tiny infant:
Continue breastfeeding your baby if you are able, even
though you have returned to work outside the home. Mothers
have confided in me that when they return home after a day's

work and are exhausted, nursing their baby relaxes them. This is probably due to the relaxing effect of the milk-producing hormones. Another advantage of breastfeeding is that it continues the bonding that you had when you were a full-time mother, maintaining the very special relationship that no one else can duplicate. Breastfeeding definitely helps the infant adjust to the change in parenting styles. In order to survive the frequent night waker, be open to trying whatever sleeping arrangement gets all three of you the most sleep. Usually working mothers find that taking the baby to bed at night helps the whole family sleep better, because baby gets the much-needed touch time at night that he missed during the day. It also makes continued breastfeeding easier by keeping your milk supply up.

Instruct the babysitter not to let the baby sleep all day, but to provide a more stimulating environment to entice baby to enjoy being awake. After all, she is a substitute mother and should mother your baby as closely as possible to the way you would during the day.

The sleep disturbances that occur when you return to work also depend upon the age of your baby. Between nine and fifteen months babies show a heightened separation anxiety. One of the developmental reasons for this is that they have not yet developed the quality of object permanency— meaning that baby cannot understand that mother still exists even though she is not there. Nighttime mothering, such as sharing sleep and nursing, helps to minimize the daytime separation anxiety.

For the older infant and child who wakes up after mother returns to work, try the following. Put a sleeping bag or futon at the foot of your bed and let the child enjoy that closeness to you at night. The child is not manipulating you.

In studying parents of large families, one of the main characteristics I have noticed is that the more children they have, the less parents worry about terms like "manipulation" and "spoiling." Listening to the child is not considered a weakness, but respect for a little person with big needs.

Try having daddy sleep with the child for a few nights if sharing sleep with your baby does not work for you (and it doesn't for some mothers because they are too sensitive and wake up too often). Part of the adjustment of mother's returning to work is to wean the baby or child from dependency on mother to a shared dependency on both parents. Be prepared for this adjustment to nighttime fathering to take a while. Baby has to adjust to father's different methods of nighttime comforting, and father has to develop his own nighttime comforting skills. It is natural for the nighttime mother to hover outside the child's bedroom door to make sure daddy is doing his job. Try to resist this tendency, as it will only cause you to be anxious and give your husband the message that you do not trust his nighttime skills.

29

SLEEP PROBLEMS IN THE SICK AND HOSPITALIZED CHILD

Any change in the child's routine, especially the trauma of being sick and hospitalized, may produce sleep problems. Here is where the art of nighttime parenting really shines. If possible, stay overnight with your child if she is in the hospital. Most hospitals now recognize the value of nighttime parenting and will offer the parents the option of a cot next to the child's bed. Children definitely get well faster when the parents share their care in the hospital. Being with your child in the hospital overnight is particularly helpful if she has breathing problems, such as croup. If a parent can relax the whole child, the breathing passages often relax—and this is especially true if you are still breastfeeding. This relationship has been the child's most trusted pacifier, one which should continue in the hospital.

To illustrate the medical importance of the mother's comforting, let me share with you my experience with a mother caring for her sick infant in the hospital. Tony was ten months old when he was hospitalized for severe croup. He was having trouble getting air into his lungs because of swollen vocal cords. This was becoming a medical emergency and we feared that a tracheostomy (a surgical opening into his windpipe) might be needed. I mentioned to Cindy, his mother, the importance of relaxing Tony so that his airway would also relax. Since Tony was an avid breastfeeder, his mother lifted up the side of the oxygen tent, leaned over Tony's crib, and comforted him with her breast. Tony relaxed, as did his airway. His breathing improved, and the operation was no longer necessary. Chalk up another point for the importance of mothers.

Comfort by parents is especially important for the sick or premature newborn. Recent studies have shown the therapeutic benefit of so-called "kangaroo care." The sick baby is wrapped around mother or father's chest and they are encouraged to sit in a chair and rock. Research has confirmed what intuitive parents have suspected all along—that touching and rocking has therapeutic value for the baby.

Sick and hospitalized newborns, especially if they undergo prolonged hospitalized stays with separation from their parents, have a higher incidence of becoming fussy babies. One of the ways to minimize this is to spend as much time as possible offering kangaroo care to your hospitalized newborn. This is especially true if the premature baby has apnea, or episodes of stopped breathing. As former director of a newborn nursery, I have noticed that when babies are draped over a parent's chest and are rocked, stroked, or sung to, their breathing becomes more regular and they have fewer apnea spells. A premature who breathes better will grow better. In fact, studies have have shown that premature infants who have kangaroo care put on weight faster and have shorter hospital stays. You are a valuable member of the medical team, and certainly at a much lower cost.

30

NIGHTMARES AND OTHER COMMON SLEEP DISORDERS

Nighttime is a scary time for little people. It is no wonder. At night they are alone; it is dark; and they are without familiar comforting resources. The most common disorders of sleep in children are nightmares, night terrors, and sleepwalking.

Nightmares are scary dreams. They occur during the REM stage of sleep (see Key 17), when a child's mind is still very active. The term "nightmare" arises from the Teutonic word *mar*, meaning devil. During the Middle Ages it was believed that nightmares were caused by a demon pressing upon the sleeper's chest. Children's dreams are usually a reenactment of their daytime experiences, good and bad. Because they have such vivid imaginations, children are prone to distort reality in their dreams; for example, a cat may appear like a tiger, and even a familiar pet may become a monster. This distorted image easily awakens the child because it occurs during the light state of sleep. The awakened child is terrified because he is not yet capable of distinguishing fantasy and dreams from reality. She believes that there really might be a monster in her room.

Sleep researchers believe that nightmares may even occur during the first year of life and definitely during the second year. Nightmares may be a reaction to emotional struggles during the day—for example, if the child is left alone with an unsuitable caregiver. Family stress, marital difficulties, a recent move, or any major change that upsets the child's equilibrium can predispose her to nightmares. Sometimes nightmares occur after a child has had an unpleasant experience, such as hospitalization or being lost in a store.

Try the following to minimize nightmares:

1. **Minimize scary experiences during the day.** Three-year-olds can often relate the content of their dreams or nightmares. Ask your child to describe the nightmare in detail so that you can pinpoint the scary daytime trigger. You may be surprised what you learn. It could be a seemingly harmless cartoon that the child watched before going to bed. I have noticed, in the last few years, an increasingly violent, almost demonic, nature to some cartoons. Cartoon makers are getting away with a lot of violence in cartoons simply because it is animation. Adults have nightmares following these cartoons; it is no wonder children do. One three-year-old patient of mine who had recurrent nightmares seemed to have an emotionally secure world. His mother said that he never watched cartoons, the parents screened everything he watched on television, and he was always with them. Upon further questioning, the cause of the nightmares emerged: the child watched the evening news and saw all the violence portrayed in the broadcast.

2. **Fight fantasy with fantasy.** If your child insists that there is a dragon in his room, play a little game with him: "Daddy went into your room and caught the dragon and put him in a

cage." Try this only as a last resort because you may be reinforcing the child's suspicions that there really are dragons. In some children this approach works, others do better with the honest approach, "There are no dragons."

3. **Have pleasant parenting-to-bed rituals.** Tell very simple, nonviolent, non-scary stories with a happy ending. Some children prefer a brief video instead of a story. Our three-year-old loved to fall asleep while watching *Lady and the Tramp.* *Avoid* scary prayers. The familiar rhyme, "Now I lay me down to sleep. . . . If I should die before I wake, I pray the Lord my soul to take" conveys the possibility that the child may not awaken in the morning. Choose happier prayers and stories (see Key 23 for bedtime story suggestions).

4. **Provide a secure sleeping environment** that minimizes the fear of going to bed. The terrified child who awakens alone may not immediately distinguish fantasy from reality. Children who sleep in the parents' bed or bedroom have fewer nightmares, and studies show that children who sleep with siblings have fewer nightmares. Nightmares are most likely to occur in the second half of the night, when dreams seem to be more frequent. Children who are prone to nightmares may often wake up in the middle of the night (before the nightmare begins) and want to spend the rest of the night in your bedroom; allow this (see Key 20 for nighttime rules and sleeping in the parents' bedroom). Sleeping the rest of the night in this secure environment may minimize nightmares. A loving and caring nighttime environment helps the child develop a healthy sleep

attitude—that sleep is not a state one fears entering into or awakening from.

Disorders of deep (non-REM) sleep include night terrors, sleepwalking, sleep talking, and bedwetting. These disorders have several features in common: there is often a family history of similar disorders; they usually occur in the first few hours after falling asleep; they are more frequent in males. The child is not completely awake during these episodes, has no memory of the event, and is very difficult to arouse during the event. The deeper the state of sleep, the more strange and frightening the child acts. Non-REM sleep disorders are not usually caused by emotional disturbances, any particular parenting style, or any underlying psychological disturbance. Though these sleep disorders are notoriously resistant to treatment, most children completely outgrow them.

Night terrors are the most frightening sleep disturbance for parents to witness. A child who has been in a state of deep sleep suddenly sits up in bed, lets out a piercing scream, thrashes about, and appears pale and terrified. He stares with his eyes wide open at an imaginary object, cries incoherently, breathes heavily, perspires, and is completely unreceptive to his parents' attempts to console him. These terrors usually last from five to ten minutes. The child is not really awake, and after the attack he falls back into a deep, calm sleep. Later he will not recall the experience. Although disturbing to the parents, night terrors do not usually appear to bother the child; because he is not fully awake when they occur, he will not remember this bizarre nighttime activity. In nightmares, on the other hand, the child does fully awaken and can remember the scary dream; he has difficulty reentering sleep without nighttime parenting.

What to do about night terrors? Nothing. Because your child does not remember them and is not fully awake, they do not usually interfere with sleep. In fact, if you try to confront or awaken your child, he may push you away or behave angrily. He does not understand your desire to help and you do not understand that he does not need help. If you do feel the need to intervene, simply offer calming, soothing words of reassurance, an "It's all right" message.

Sleepwalking also bothers parents more than children. During sleepwalking a child appears clumsy, but surprisingly is coordinated enough to steer around obstacles without falling or injuring himself. Doors and drawers are often opened. The child's nighttime rounds may last from five to thirty minutes, and then he returns to bed without any recall of where he went or what he did. Because this occurs during the state of deep sleep, the sleepwalker is very difficult to arouse, although one-third of the episodes do terminate with the child awakening.

Some sleepwalkers have accompanying night terrors. Although sleepwalkers seldom hurt themselves, it is wise to create a safe environment in which your little sleeper can walk. Eliminate hazardous objects from the sleeping stroller's path—sharp-edged furniture, electric cords, vaporizers, space heaters, etc. If your nocturnal navigator manages to get out of his own bedroom and awaken you, try to gently guide him back into bed rather than attempting to awaken him fully.

Sleep talking may accompanying sleepwalking. The speech during sleep can be surprisingly intelligible, and the content of the talk is usually related to the experiences of the preceding day. If you have the urge to eavesdrop it is sometimes the best way to know what is occupying your child's mind.

With time, maturing, a bit of humor, and a touch of nighttime parenting these nocturnal nuisances disappear.

31

~~~~~~

NIGHTTIME HABITS

During sleep infants will often revert to longstanding habits as conscious or semiconscious self-soothing techniques. Sleep is a regressive state; during periods of need, tiny infants return to a familiar pattern of comfort.

Thumbsucking is the most familiar nighttime habit, as the ever-present thumb is a ready pacifier for the sleeping infant. Some infants and children cannot drift off to sleep without the comfort of their thumbs. Some children suck their thumbs habitually during most of the night. The majority of children suffer no ill effects from nighttime thumbsucking, but the occasional child may put enough pressure on his upper front teeth to cause an overbite that needs orthodontic repair. Thumbsucking usually causes an overbite—protrusion of the upper teeth over the lower. Fingersucking, on the other hand, produces an underbite in which the lower teeth protrude over the upper. If your child does not have any dental deformities secondary to thumbsucking, allow this habit to gradually subside. Like most childhood habits, it too will pass. If your doctor or dentist diagnoses dental deformities caused by the thumbsucking, try to observe when during the night cycle your child habitually sucks his thumb. If it is while going to sleep, then he needs to fall asleep using a different pacifier.

Consider for a moment the meaning of the term "pacifier"—something that brings peace. This is exactly what a child needs when going through the transition from the state of being awake to the state of sleep—something that brings a peaceful transition. This is why children will often use the most available and familiar pacifier—their thumb, if it is all that's available. If you want or need to break the nighttime thumbsucking habit, change pacifiers. An alternative is to get an artificial pacifier that the child hugs and grabs rather than sucks, such as a cuddly bear or a furry toy (if your child is not allergic). I advise bears that are large enough for the child to wrap his arm around without being able to reach his thumb. Another alternative is mom or dad. An occasional mother in my practice has complained, "I don't want to be a human pacifier!" Is it wrong to constantly nurse him off to sleep at the breast? No, it is not wrong, it is very right. Isn't it beautiful that a child can consider his favorite human beings his pacifiers—those that bring peace. These are beautiful memories that I'm sure are stored within the child and periodically retrieved throughout the rest of his life as he reflects upon how his parents raised him.

Researchers studied fifty children between the ages of one and seven who habitually sucked their thumbs, comparing them with a control group who did not. The studies showed that thumbsuckers tended to be bottle-fed rather than breastfed. The later the child was weaned, the less likely he was to suck his thumb. The thumbsucking children tended to have been fed on schedule rather than on demand. Most significant was the finding that 96% of the thumbsuckers had been left to fall asleep alone after having been fed. Among the children who did not suck their thumbs, there was not a single child who was left to fall asleep alone. Instead, these children were given the opportunity to suck until they fell asleep.

Sleep is a regressive activity during which there is a return to more primitive reflexes, such as sucking and hand-to-mouth actions. As he falls asleep the child's primitive sucking reflex is stimulated and the sucking drive is intensified.

Researchers theorize that if the infant goes to sleep while sucking at the breast, bottle, or pacifier, the sucking drive will be satisfied and the hand-to-mouth reflex will not stimulate sucking later in the night. In other words, a need filled in early infancy disappears. A need that is not filled does not go away but reappears, sometimes as an undesirable habit. In my own practice I have noticed that babies who are nursed down to sleep, offered unrestricted night nursing, and are not weaned until they are ready are much less likely to become habitual thumbsuckers.

Some babies, regardless of the style of nighttime parenting, have a tremendous need to suck and will be habitual nighttime thumbsuckers. Many of these babies develop no dental abnormalities and gradually drop the habit within the first two years. These thumbsuckers are born, not made. Ultrasound studies have shown that babies even suck their thumbs in utero. I have pictures of one of our newborns sucking his thumb five minutes after birth.

Unless artificial pacifiers or thumbsucking are causing a dental problem, do not discourage them. Sometimes a child needs this tension releaser, and if the habit is "broken" the child releases tension in more objectionable types of behavior, usually in discipline problems or temper tantrums. Everyone at all ages has pacifiers. Think of how many things we as adults do—we chew, suck, smoke—all to derive pleasure and/or relieve tension. Should a child be deprived of his own pacifiers when adults need not be?

Tooth grinding (the dental term is bruxism) makes an annoying sound and is a potentially detrimental nighttime habit. Even before the first tooth comes in, some infants mash their upper and lower gums together while sleeping. Dentists think this is a muscular habit that serves as a tension-releasing device. Depending on the number of teeth, a tooth-grinding child can make a lot of very annoying noise.

Some tooth grinding can be a sign of allergies; the child may be using muscular contortions of the jaw to open the eustachian tube and relax middle-ear pressure that may have built up because of allergies. I have seen tooth grinding go away when the allergies are treated properly. Some dentists are able to treat both tooth grinding and habitual thumb-sucking by insertion of an appliance that fits into the mouth and discourages these habits. These appliances serve more as reminders than preventatives. With the appliance, the thumb or the tooth grinding just doesn't feel the way it used to.

Night waking for a bottle. After the infant has four to six teeth (usually around one year of age), it is wise to discourage anything but water for a nighttime bottle. The sugars in milk, formula, and especially juice can cause tooth decay, called bottle-mouth caries, because during sleep there is decreased saliva and thus less natural rinsing action in the mouth. For the child who is a habitual nighttime milk or juice drinker, try the trick of "watering down"—gradually water down the juice or milk until it becomes mostly water. It is wise to brush the child's teeth as soon as he awakens in the morning.

32

BEDWETTING

Why does your child wet his bed? I want to emphasize that for the great majority of children, bedwetting is *not* due to a psychological disturbance. For most children, the problem is due to immaturity of the bladder, not of the mind. Current research also places bedwetting in the category of a sleep disorder.

It may help to understand why your child wets his or her bed by first understanding how a child reaches bladder maturity. Infants have what is called a "bladder-emptying reflex." When the bladder reaches a certain fullness and its muscles have stretched to a certain point, they automatically contract and empty the bladder. Sometime between the ages of eighteen months and two years, most children become aware of this sensation of bladder fullness; they can feel it coming but can't stop it. The next step in bladder maturity is for the child to become aware that he can consciously inhibit the bladder-emptying reflex and hold onto his urine. As a result of this conscious effort, the child's bladder-emptying reflex weakens and the functional capacity of his bladder increases. When his conscious efforts overcome the bladder-emptying reflex, he achieves daytime bladder control—usually between two and two and a half years of age.

Nighttime control occurs when the child's bladder capacity increases and the bladder-emptying reflex becomes so weak that it can be overcome by unconscious inhibition of urination. Delay in bladder control, either daytime or nighttime, can occur if any of these steps is delayed—the awareness of bladder fullness, the increase in bladder capacity, or the weakening of the bladder-emptying reflex. Just as children mature at different rates, the components of bladder control also mature at different rates.

At what age should parents be concerned about bedwetting? There is tremendous variation in the age at which children remain dry throughout the night. By three years, most children are dry at night; at six years of age, 92% of girls and 85 to 90% of boys remain dry at night. Pediatricians usually consider bedwetting after the age of six a condition meriting correction. What is more important is the age at which the child himself is concerned.

Heredity is probably the single most important factor influencing bedwetting. If both parents were bedwetters, the child has a 70% chance of being a bedwetter; if one parent was a bedwetter, the child has a 40% chance.

Bedwetting and sleep. Parents of bedwetters often mention that their children are very sound sleepers. Some studies suggest that bedwetters do not sleep more soundly than dry children; other studies suggest that bedwetting is truly a sleep disorder in many children. Most bedwetting occurs one to three hours after falling asleep, as a child ascends from deep sleep into the first cycle of light, or REM, sleep. Some bedwetters have different sleep cycles than children who are dry at night. Bedwetting children descend into a deep sleep quickly and remain in the state of deep sleep longer. The first bedwetting episode of the night occurs near the end of this prolonged period of deep sleep, before the first REM period. This sequence explains why many children awaken at the first REM period to find themselves already wet. During this prolonged deep sleep stage the brain is unaware that the bladder is full and needs help. Bedwetting later in the night usually occurs during a period of light, or REM, sleep, perhaps because of the generalized increase in muscle tone and bladder-muscle contractions as the child ascends out of deep sleep. Studies have shown that bedwetters have more frequent and stronger bladder contractions during deep sleep than do other children.

In some children, bedwetting may actually be a sleep disorder in which the loss of bladder control occurs as the child passes from one sleep stage to another. It is a known anatomical fact that children who wet their beds have functionally small bladders and must void more frequently. This fact, plus the hereditary basis, suggests that bedwetting is not due to a psychological disturbance. In the majority of children, bedwetting should be considered a developmental delay in one or more of the components of bladder control.

Medical causes of bedwetting. In a very small percentage of children bedwetting may be due to a medical cause. It is wise not to assume that your child's bedwetting is a sleep or maturity disorder until a medical cause has been excluded. Have a routine urinalysis and urine culture done on two or three occasions. Signs that may lead you to suspect a medical problem are frequent urinary infections, dribbling, incontinence, frequent strong urges to urinate, painful urination, daytime wetness, and bedwetting that resists conventional treatment.

Food allergies have been implicated as a cause of bedwetting, although many of these claims have not been substantiated. In some children dairy allergies may have contributed to bedwetting, as have binges on highly sugared junk foods and artificial food colorings. Caffeine-containing foods and drinks (colas, tea, coffee, and chocolate) may contribute to bedwetting.

138

Environmental and emotional influences. Bedwetting is much more frequent during emotional stress, family upset, or following a major change such as a move or the death of a loved one. This is understandable, since these factors also disturb normal sleep patterns.

Treating bedwetting. Bedwetting is one of the least understood and most undertreated problems in nighttime parenting. The degree to which bedwetting bothers the child is underestimated. Bedwetting is more than just a wet child; sleep fragmentation and the social stigma of bedwetting may adversely affect a child's behavior and self-esteem. To help your child achieve dry nights, try the following:

1. **Organize the child's sleep patterns.** Treatment of bedwetting begins with helping a child achieve normal light-sleep cycles. Minimize daytime stress. Anxiety, stress, and general unright feelings during the day can disturb sleep. This may account for the increased frequency of bedwetting during periods of adjustment in a child's life, such as starting school, the birth of a sibling, a move, or the death of a family member. A child who feels right is more likely to sleep well.

   Minimize nighttime stress. A disturbed child is likely to have disturbed sleep. Even an older child may not feel right sleeping alone in a room. I have noticed that some children will cease bedwetting when they are allowed to sleep on a mattress next to their parents' bed. This may account for the well-known observation that children wet their beds less during overnight visits with friends or while traveling, either of which often necessitates sharing a bed. Encourage order in the child's life. To achieve regularity in sleep cycles, it is often necessary to create regularity in the child's daily schedule—more consistent mealtimes, naptimes, rising times, and bedtimes. Specialists in the treatment of bedwetting have found that consistent and earlier bedtimes help most children achieve better nighttime bladder control.

2. **Motivate the child.** Encourage overnights at friends' houses and overnight camps. Encouraging him to take along his own overnight pad and sleeping bag may relieve some embarrassment. It helps to prepare the parents at his friend's house so that they can be equally understanding and supportive. Chances are they also have parented a bedwetter.

If your child is a prolonged bedwetter, make a special effort to encourage success in other fields of development, such as academics or athletics. He should not feel like he is a total failure. I have noticed a carryover effect; when children excel in one or more things, their immature areas often rapidly mature. Motivate your child to assist with the laundry and to strip his own bed, not as a punishment but as a means to convey to him a sense of responsibility for his bodily functions. Placing a large rubber-backed flannel pad on top of his regular sheet may cut down on the number of wet sheets.

3. **Bladder exercises.** Some physicians recommend bladder exercises to increase the functional capacity of the child's bladder and the muscular control of his bladder during the day, in hopes that this will carry over into his subconscious awareness of bladder control at night. Two examples of bladder-control exercises are progressive urine withholding and the stop-and-go. For progressive urine withholding, encourage

your child to drink increasing amounts of fluid and to hold onto his urine for longer and longer. Theoretically, this increases his functional bladder capacity and weakens the bladder-emptying reflex. To practice the stop-and-go technique, have the child stop the stream several times during urination. This increases his awareness that he can actually control his "donut muscle" if he really wants to. Bladder-control exercises are usually more productive for children who have difficulty controlling their urine during the day; discuss the problem with the child's physician before using them.

4. **Teach your child the principles of bladder control** and explain to him why he wets the bed. Your child does not want to wet his bed. He dislikes waking up in a malodorous bed as much as you dislike constantly changing and washing his sheets. Older children are painfully aware of the social stigma accompanying bedwetting; they do not need further negative attitudes from their parents. Explain to your child how his bladder mechanism works. Draw a simple diagram of a baseball as a bladder, and at the bottom of the ball show the "donut muscle" that opens and closes to help him hold onto his urine. Tell him he is not a baby now, but his bladder and his donut muscle have not grown up yet and he needs to work hard to keep the donut muscle closed at night. It is important that your child does not feel like he is a baby in everything.

I am not suggesting that you ignore bedwetting, especially in the child older than five or six, since it is a source of embarrassment and certainly does nothing to help his emerging self-esteem. As you would with other childhood behaviors, convey a supportive attitude toward your child. When his subconscious desire to hold onto his urine overcomes the bladder's reflex to let go, he will enjoy nighttime dryness.

5. **Restricting fluids after supper** is one of the oldest recommended practices for discouraging bedwetting. In my experience it seldom does any good and is uncomfortable for the persistently thirsty child. Food and drinks that contain caffeine should be avoided, since caffeine acts as a diuretic and actually may contribute to bedwetting.

6. **The shake-and-wake method** is the old custom of waking your child before you go to bed so he can urinate. If you go to the trouble to get your child out of bed, be sure you awaken him completely so he can walk to the toilet on his own power. In order to clarify to your child that you are not taking the primary responsibility for his nocturnal toileting, ask if he wants you to wake him up before you go to bed. If he is willing, then this practice may be worth a trial.

7. **Medications for bedwetting.** Medications for control of bedwetting may be given to a child a half-hour before bedtime. Medications are thought to improve bladder muscle control and affect the state of sleep by allowing the child to be more aware of his bladder fullness. There are also nasal sprays that affect the hormones which control urination and bladder functioning. For most children, medications are less safe and effective than bladder-conditioning devices. Re-

lapses are also more common after the medications are stopped. In my opinion, medications should not be used to control bedwetting until all other methods discussed here have been tried and your doctor makes the decision that your child's bedwetting problems have an adverse effect on his general self-esteem.

Dr. Bill's bedwetting regimen. Over my eighteen years in practice I have struggled with a variety of bedwetting regimens, some successful, some not. Here's the one that I have found most successful in treating most bedwetters most of the time.

1. **Provide an anatomical explanation.** Have a conference with the child and ask him if he wants help, for you are asking his permission to get into his private life a bit. If the answer is yes, proceed with an explanation of why he wets his bed, drawing diagrams. I draw a diagram of the brain and of the bladder. I explain how during the day the brain and the bladder talk to each other; when the bladder is full it tells the brain, and the brain sends a message to the bladder to let go. At night, because the brain is asleep, it doesn't listen to the bladder, so the key is to help the brain hear the bladder at night. I also put in the diagram of the donut muscle, which I mentioned above. During this first visit I also do a routine urinalysis and medical history, looking for any signs alerting me to a medical problem. If there is a family history of bedwetting I offer the reassuring comment, "Your father and his doctor probably had this same talk thirty years ago."

2. **Teach the child how to completely empty his bladder before going to bed.** Little children,

tired and in a hurry, often go to the toilet, dribble a little and run off to resume play or go to bed with a half-full bladder. Encourage a triple voiding technique before going to bed. Tell the child to grunt and void, wait about ten seconds, grunt and void again, then a third time.

3. **Try a bladder-conditioning device.** In my experience this is the most safe and effective method of helping the child achieve nighttime bladder control. Several of these devices are commercially available. They consist of a pad that the child wears inside his underwear at night. The pad is connected by a wire to a tiny buzzer that fastens to the child's pajamas. When a drop or two of urine hits the moisture-sensitive pad, a beep sounds and wakes the child to complete his urination in the toilet. The device operates on the principle that the child's own bladder-fullness sensor is not sufficient to awaken him fully, but the stimulus of the beep alarm is. Your child will learn to associate the feelings he had just before urination with awakening, so that in time he awakens at the first urge to urinate—before the alarm sounds (we call this "beat the beeper").

For the device to be effective, parent and child must undergo two to three weeks of before-bedtime drills in which the following steps are observed: 1. Triple void; 2. Rehearse what the child will do when the beeper goes off.

Put the child to bed with his pad and buzzer on. Sound the alarm and encourage the child to jump out of bed, walk to the toilet, turn the faucet on, splash cool water on his face so he is fully awakened, and then void in the toilet. Then repeat this same drill three times before going to bed. This implants in the child's mind before he retires the sequence that he is supposed to duplicate during the night, so that he knows exactly what to do when the beeper goes off. Also use a calendar with wet and dry stars; after a certain number of dry stars he gets a reward. I also have the children call me (the parent dials the number but the child actually talks to me and reports in weekly how he is doing).

After two to three weeks of this drill, most children will report they frequently "beat the beeper." Some sleep so deeply that the beeper wakes up everyone else in the house but not the child; if this happens, get a louder beeper. If the child still sleeps through it, leave the beeper going and awaken the child to turn it off himself. He can go to the bathroom to urinate and then reset the alarm. Relapses are common after this treatment, and a second course may be necesary to achieve permanent success. I suggest that you try all the steps in this nighttime drill and discuss the use of the bladder-conditioning device with your doctor.

33

~~~~~~

HANDLING CRITICISM

When you have a new baby be prepared for a parade of well-meaning advisors offering their personal how-to's of baby care. This deluge of unsolicited advice comes at a time when parents are most vulnerable. During the first month nearly every new mother is naturally a bit shaky in her confidence. Be prepared for such admonitions as, "You'll spoil the baby," "You're holding him too much," "Let her cry it out," etc., etc.

He's your baby, no one else's. Developing the right fit with your baby means matching the lifestyle and giving level of the parent to the temperament and need level of the baby. You may have a different lifestyle than your advisor. You are obviously a different person than your advisor, and your baby is certainly different than your advisor's baby. Books and advisors must generalize; you and your baby are individuals. Beware of "You should." They are not you, and *should* is a judgment call.

In handling criticism it helps to remember where your advisors are coming from. They are often parents from a past generation—your mother, mother-in-law, or relative. Parenting styles of the '50s and '60s were different. This was the era in which the fear of spoiling and being manipulated scared the basic intuition out of mothers. Parents were counseled against holding their babies too much, feeding their babies too often, and carrying their babies a lot, and were certainly advised not to sleep with their babies. This was the era of detachment parenting; mothers turned over their basic intuitive feelings to advisors and authority figures. Most of the books preached detachment. Babies were separated from mothers at birth, at the breast, and at night. The '80s and '90s, on the contrary, may be known as the attachment era. Today's mother is more confident in her own intuition. Studies have shown that the detachment philosophy benefits neither mothers nor babies. Today's parents read more, prepare better, and choose their health care providers and advisors more selectively. It is not that your advisors are malicious; this was the way they were taught and how they parented. It is only because babies possess the quality of resilience that most infants came through this detachment period apparently all right.

Appear confident and satisfied with your parenting style. Nothing turns off oversolicitous advisors like a parent's success. When they see that what you are doing is working for you, they will back off. In fact, one way to ward off criticizers is the simple statement, "It's working for me!" Don't feel you have to defend your position to anybody. Grandmother had her shot; this is your baby. In fact, one of the best ways to build up confidence is by explaining your views to parents who do not share the same style of parenting.

Surround yourself with like-minded parents. Nothing divides friends like different views toward parenting. Selecting friends who validate your style of mothering will increase your confidence that what you are doing is right for your baby and yourself. Studies have shown that new mothers are bothered most by criticism from their husbands, from their own mothers, from their mother-in-law, and from people who don't have children. The best way to win over your husband is if he sees that what you are doing is working. Throwing out periodic confident statements such as, "I feel right about it" may also win over a skeptical husband who is still trying to find out what "mother's intuition" really means. He may never understand it but he may grow to respect it.

To win over mothers and mothers-in-law, don't set yourself up for confrontation. If you sense their disapproval of your mothering style, avoid even mentioning it. If you know they would be aghast if you sleep with your baby, don't tell them. If a confrontation occurs, use authority figures as scapegoats: "My doctor advised me to ..." or "Did you see the article about why it is not good to let babies cry...." This may catch your advisor off-guard—she may not want to appear less knowledgeable than you—and you are showing that you care enough about your parenting style to seek advice. Remember, your mother and mother-in-law came from the era of "experts." They were vulnerable to what the doctor said. Today's child-rearing "experts" have taken another approach, to offer parents the tools for becoming their own experts. This is the approach I have taken in this book.

34

~~~~~~

SINGLE NIGHTTIME PARENTING

Sleep disturbances follow a divorce, a death, or prolonged parental absence. When the harmony of a two-parent family (even one in which there has been marital discord) is interrupted, a child's behavior is disrupted, especially his sleep cycles. Naptimes become more unpredictable, bedtime rituals more prolonged, and night waking more frequent. Coping with these nighttime stresses is particularly difficult for the single parent who is also going through some readjustments in getting his or her own life back together.

Helping your child sleep better. Be consistent. Try to minimize the changes in your child's life as much as possible; don't switch home, neighborhood, beds, or babysitters. Babies and children of all ages get used to the family routine, and too many changes too fast are guaranteed to produce a night waker.

Naptime difficulties are usually encountered in addition to frequent night waking. Besides the change in the secure environment after a divorce or separation, the child is now very likely sleeping at two different homes and is expected to adapt his sleep rhythm to two different lifestyles. It is common for children not to sleep well in either home. The child may awaken frequently at the custodial parent's home out of fear that this parent may also leave. He awakens frequently at the noncustodial parent's home because he is required to sleep in a different bed and is sometimes not

149

permitted to sleep with the parent, which he may be accustomed to do at his more familiar home.

Expect signs of insecurity. Following the breakup of a marriage it is very common for a child to cling to the custodial parent, mainly because of fear that this parent may also leave. It is usual for children not to want to nap alone, go to bed alone, or sleep alone. Even tiny babies sense the change in the family routine. Because mother is upset, this is transmitted to even the newborn baby and can account for sleep disturbances. Fears often keep the older child awake—"What will happen next?" Blaming themselves, the worry that they caused daddy to leave also keeps children awake.

Be open to your child's cues that he needs security. It is very normal and healthy for a previously independent child to be glued to mommy now. If your baby or toddler wants to sleep with you, welcome her into your bed at least for a few months during the adjustment period. For the older child, a mattress alongside your bed will usually suffice. Remember, though, that a child is not a substitue for an absent mate; the co-sleeping arrangement fulfills the needs of the child, not the adult. Older children are especially sensitive to the custodial parent leaning on them for security when they themselves are insecure. A certain amount of this mutual support is normal in single-parent families, as long as a healthy balance is achieved.

When the child sleeps in the noncustodial parent's home, it helps to take a familiar attachment object along, such as a lambskin sleep mat, a favorite blanket, or a teddy bear. If the young child is used to sleeping with the custodial parent, continue this sleeping arrangement with the other parent if comfortable. Both parents need to agree on consistent naptimes, bedtimes, and sleeping arrangements.

Anticipate that the most difficult sleep problems will occur on the night that the child changes homes. The custodial parent will often report that, "After a weekend with daddy it took several nights to get him to sleep through again." One of the reasons for this sleep disturbance is the different lifestyles in the two homes. The custodial parent, usually the mother, is required to be the disciplinarian and usually runs a tighter ship with consistent naptimes and bedtimes. The noncustodial parent, usually the father, may assume the role of "Disneyland daddy" and create an undisciplined environment of junk food and unstructured naptimes. This confusion of lifestyles upsets the already confused child, who requires several days to adjust. Some mutual agreement on maintaining a consistency of lifestyles will help lessen this confusion and help the child to sleep better.

35

THE PAYOFF

How do high-need babies turn out? What is the long term effect of the attachment-style parenting that I suggest throughout this book? I have had the opportunity to study the effects of attachment parenting in thousands of patients over the years, as well as in our own children. While no parents are able to practice the attachments style of parenting all the time, we have observed that children reared with the attachment style of parenting tend to show a number of desirable qualities, as do their parents. Among these qualities are:

Sensitivity. The main quality I notice in attachment-parented babies is sensitivity. Because they grow up in a sensitive and responsive environment, this is the attitude they develop. Because their early caregivers were sensitive to their needs, these children are sensitive to others' needs. They are generally bothered when another child is hurt. They are concerned about the needs and rights of others. One of the moral disasters we see in many children is that nothing bothers them. Insensitivity gets them—and us—into trouble. Many social ills, even wars, can be traced to one group's insensitivity to another.

Giving. These little takers become big givers because they grow up in a giving environment. Believe it or not, they learn to share more easily—a trait that comes hard to many children. Attachment parents have achieved a balance in their giving, neither indulging nor restraining.

Good discipline. When children feel right, operate from a basis of trust, and are not angry, they are easier to discipline. Attachment parenting really pays off for the high-need baby who, by nature, is at risk of becoming an impulsive child. This unbridled impulsiveness is what gets them into trouble.

High self-esteem. Attachment-parented children become satisfied with people rather than things. They become personally bonded children in a materialistic world. They are high-touch children, not high-tech children. They strive for deep interpersonal relationships.

There's also a payoff for the next generation. Parents, keep in mind that you are bringing up someone else's future husband or wife, father or mother. The parenting styles that your child learns from you are the ones he is most likely to follow when he becomes a parent. Modeling begins at a very young age. One day a mother brought in her newborn, Tiffany, for a checkup, accompanied by three-year-old Erin, the product of attachment parenting. As soon as Tiffany started to fuss, Erin pulled at her mother's skirt, saying with much emotion, "Mommy, Tiffany cry; pickup, rock-rock, nurse." Is it hard to guess what Erin will do someday when her own baby cries? She won't call her doctor. She won't look it up in a book. She will intuitively pick up, rock-rock, and nurse.

Even teenagers pick up on your style of parenting. One day Martha and I were sitting in our family room when we heard our nine-month-old daughter, Erin, crying in our bedroom. As we got near the door, the cries stopped. Curious, we looked into see why Erin had stopped crying, and what we saw left a warm feeling in our hearts. Jim, our sixteen-year-old athlete, was lying next to Erin, stroking and gentling her. Why did Jim do this? Because he was following our modeling that when babies cry, someone listens and responds.

Parents reap benefits from attachment parenting too. The main effect may be summed up in one word: *harmony.* This beautiful term is what attachment parenting is all about. There are various dictionary definitions of harmony, but the simplest and the one I like best is "getting along well together." Attachment parents whom I have interviewed make these statements:

"I feel so connected to my child."
"I feel right when I'm with him,
   not right when we are apart."
"I feel complete."

These are the real bonding effects of attachment parenting.

QUESTIONS AND ANSWERS

Q. We are expecting our first baby in a month and are trying to decide where he or she should sleep. Is it okay to sleep with our baby?

A normal fact of nighttime parenting life is that you will do a lot of juggling of sleeping arrangements during your baby's first year. My advice is that wherever all three of you, mother, father, and baby, sleep the best is the right arrangement for you. Be open to trying various arrangements. Openness is the key to nighttime parenting—in fact, to all parenting. I advise you to begin sleeping with your baby right after you come home from the hospital. This allows you and your baby to harmonize sleep cycles with each other, makes nighttime nursing easier, lessens night waking, and generally gives you and your baby that extra touch time. Be prepared for your baby to wake up frequently anyway. The key is to minimize her waking and get her back to sleep as easily as you can, preferably without even waking up yourself. Having a baby sleep with you in your own bed does not always work, but I advise you to try it. If it works, continue this beautiful arrangement.

Q. We would like to have our new baby sleep with us, but my doctor advises us not to. I'm confused. Who is right?

There are three questions you should *not* ask your doctor: "Where should my baby sleep?" "How long should my baby nurse?" and "Should I let my baby cry it out?" Doctors do not study the answers to these questions in medical school, and much of their advice comes from their own personal experience as mothers and fathers, not as professionals. You are putting doctors on the spot when you ask them where your baby should sleep. Doctors are trained in the diagnosis and treatment of illnesses, not in parenting styles. If you want to sleep with your baby and feel that your baby, your husband, and you will all sleep better with this nighttime parenting style, this is the right decision for your family. Incidentally, you will find that in recent years doctors have become increasingly flexible about parents sleeping with their babies. Doctors are now realizing that they will not have to spend so much time counseling parents about sleep problems later on if the parents spend more time helping their baby form a healthy sleep attitude in the early months.

Q. I have a fussy baby and he is very comforted by nursing. How long should I nurse him?

You probably have a high-need baby. The needs of these special babies are not only higher but longer. Expect your baby to want to nurse for one or two years, and sometimes even longer. Also be prepared for comments like, "What, you're still nursing?" Just like weaning from the parents' bed, weaning from the breast should be done gradually and at a time when both members of the nursing pair are ready. In my pediatric practice I have studied many high-need babies who were breastfed for several years. In general, they turn out to be very secure and independent children. As with all other parenting styles, if prolonged nursing is working for you and your baby and feels right to you, then don't put a time limit on this beautiful relationship. Your child will not nurse off to college.

Q. I love to pick up our baby every time he cries and I hold him a lot, but I'm afraid I may be spoiling him. Is this true?

No! Research has finally disproven the old spoiling theory, putting it on the shelf forever. You cannot spoil your baby by giving a nurturant response to her cry or by carrying her a lot. There was a time when it was feared that babies who were closely attached to their parents would grow up clingy and dependent. Research shows the opposite to be true: babies who are the product of the attachment style of parenting that I advocate throughout this book actually turn out to be less clingy and more independent because they have learned to trust their environment. It is important to take a balanced approach to caring for your baby, being neither overindulgent nor insensitively restrictive. There will be times when your baby does not want to be carried and enjoys freestyle movements on the floor. There will be times when you will feel right in lengthening your response time and not running immediately to pick up your crying baby. Parents have to develop this wisdom on their own. Begin by giving an immediate nurturant response to your baby's cry, and with time you will develop the wisdom of knowing which cries to respond to immediately and which can be held off a bit. This is how you become a sensitive parent and your baby becomes a trusting child.

Q: I have recently gone back to work and find that I am often so tense and wide awake at night that I can't get to sleep. I have also noticed that my three-month-old son wakes up often, so neither one of us can get a decent night's sleep. What can I do?

Here is a good example of the concept of mutual giving. Take your baby to bed with you and nurse him off to sleep. Something good happens to both of you when you sleep and nurse next to each other. Researchers have recently discovered that your milk contains a sleep-inducing substance. When you breastfeed at night you are helping put baby to sleep. The other side of the nighttime parenting equation is that when your baby nurses he stimulates the hormone prolactin to enter your bloodstream. This hormone acts as a natural tranquilizer that helps put you to sleep. Many working mothers have shared with me that night nursing really helps them sleep better after a tough day at work.

Q: I have heard that fussy babies often turn out to be hyperactive children. Is this true?

It is not always the case, but yes, there is a general tendency for fussy babies to become hyperactive children. Because of this correlation I stress the importance of recognizing the high-need baby very early in infancy and developing a parenting style that mellows the temperament of the baby and improves the sensitivity of the parents. Needs met early in infancy often go away later. Unmet needs may surface later in undesirable behaviors. Hyperactive children are prone to becoming angry children. The attachment style of parenting I advocate throughout this book, including such practices as responding promptly to your baby's cries and holding her a lot, creates a trusting attitude within your child so she grows up less prone to anger. A child who operates from a basis of trust is less likely to become an angry, difficult-to-manage hyperactive child. A child who is hyperactive by temperament but who has grown up in a trusting environment will generally be much easier to parent.

Q. Our one-year-old screams a lot. How can we stop this behavior?

Most babies go through a screaming stage, but they are not intentionally trying to annoy. One reason why babies scream is that they love to try out their voices, and to see the effect of ear-piercing sounds on their adult listeners. We have solved the screaming problem in our children in the following two ways. First we try to identify what circumstances trigger the screaming. Usually it is a situation in which the baby's needs or wants are being ignored and he uses this screaming to attract attention. For example, if your baby screams while you are on the phone, anticipate this and engage him in an interesting activity before you make your phone call, such as giving him his own toy phone to play with. The second way in which we have handled screaming is by taking the child outside as soon as he starts to scream and saying, "We only scream on the grass," teaching him that screaming in any place but outdoors in unacceptable. As soon as your baby develops the verbal skills to communicate his needs, the screaming will subside. Like most undesirable behaviors of infancy, this too will pass.

Q: Our one-and-a-half-year-old throws a tantrum when it is time to leave a play activity. She gets so involved in what she is doing that I literally have to drag her away. Help!

Babies become so involved in play that they don't want to give it up without a fight. Here's how to lessen these departure hassles. If your baby is intensely involved in one of her favorite activities, begin to wind up the activity at least five or ten minutes before departure time. To suddenly interrupt her favorite play guarantees a protest. Gradually close out the activity by appropriate departure gestures, such as: "Bye-bye truck, bye-bye (name of friend), bye-bye blocks," etc. High-need children often have strong wills, especially when they are engaged in play. By encouraging your baby to use these departure gestures you are helping the normally strong-willed child to close out her own activites.

Q. Our baby sleeps with us and we really enjoy it, but sometimes he wakes up in the middle of the night bright-eyed, bushy-tailed and ready to play. Intitially this was fun, but now we are tired of it. How can I stop this night-time habit?

Babies need some nighttime conditioning. They need to learn that a bed is for sleeping, not for playing. We have solved this nighttime nuisance in our family by "playing dead." When our baby wakes up eager to play, we pretend that we're still asleep and ignore his desire to play. Initially this is tough to do, since your baby will probably start to crawl all over you just trying to get your attention. If you persist long enough, though, he will eventually get the message that nighttime is for sleeping.

This is not the same as letting your baby cry; babies seldom cry for play. Your baby is secure because you are there; his wanting to play is a whim, not a need. A bit of nighttime humor is also necessary to help you survive your 3:00 A.M. playmate.

Q. Our two-year-old is ready to leave our bedroom, and I'm trying to decide whether it's best to get him his own room or let him sleep with his older brother. Any suggestions?

If your child has been accustomed to sleeping close to someone, it is unlikely that he will sleep well in his own room, even snuggled up with something like a teddy bear. Part of the normal nighttime weaning is to coax a toddler from the parents' bed into a sibling's room and then into his own room. Studies have shown that children under three sleep better sharing a bedroom rather than on their own. We have also noticed that siblings who sleep together quarrel less. Watch for your child's cues that he is ready for his own room. Most children around three years old desire some private space for many of their personal belongings. A child's own room helps foster a sense of order and a sense of responsibility in caring for his own belongings. Construct low shelves, compartments for toys, and pegs for hanging clothes. An additional word of advice: I don't think separate bedrooms are important enough to warrant becoming overextended financially to buy a larger house.

Q. Our one-year-old used to sleep very well, but now she's beginning to wake up more frequently. I go and find her standing up in her crib as if she wants to get out. Why is she doing this and what should I do?

Night waking frequently occurs when babies have developed a new major developmental skill, such as going from sitting to crawling (at around six to seven months) and from crawling to walking (at around one year). Babies wake up and are so aware of their newfound skill that they want to practice it even at night. For the beginning walker, the confines of the crib may be somewhat restrictive. When you go to your baby, try to resettle her with a minimum of fuss. Put a rocking chair next to her crib and try to rock her back to sleep. If you can, get her to resettle without getting her out of the crib; even better, try getting her to lie down and pat her or massage her while singing to her. Several ingenious mothers have shared this tip with me: they lower the side rail to the level of the mattress, bend over, and nurse the baby while she is still lying in the crib. This often resettles baby without the need to pick her up out of the crib. Night waking due to the development of a new motor skill usually subsides once this skill is mastered.

Q. I have read a lot about the family bed. Many of my friends let their babies sleep in their beds, but quite honestly I just don't want to. We have four children, and by

the time evening comes I've had enough of kids. I want some time alone with my husband. Am I wrong to feel this way?

I support your feelings. You honestly feel that for your particular family situation, it is necessary for you to have this special time with your husband at night to nurture the marriage, recharge your own batteries and be a more effective mother by day. This decision is not selfish but represents a frank appraisal that the whole family will probably function better if you have separate sleeping arrangements. It sounds like you have realistic expectations of your own needs and also that you are probably blessed with a baby who is not particularly separation-sensitive at night. The best sleeping arrangement for one family may not be the best for another. My advice is that wherever all members of the family sleep the best and feel right is the best sleeping arrangement for the family. Don't feel pressured into a nighttime parenting style that you don't believe in simply because your friends do it.

Q. I am expecting a baby in a month, and our three-year-old is still sleeping with us. I don't want to exile her from our bed, but I honestly feel I can't handle two kids at night.

Making room for a new baby while another child is already in your bed is indeed a problem. In my experience, having more than one child in your bed at one time doesn't work. This is why I do not use the term "family bed," which conjures up the image of a lot of kids in one small bed and dad somewhere on the floor or the living room couch.

The problem is persuading your three-year-old to accept an alternative without feeling banished from her nighttime place of security. Remember, weaning your child from your bed means that you must substitute alternate forms of comfort and nighttime nourishment. As you mother your newborn at night, ask your husband to father the three-year-old. Treat this as something special: "Daddy and you are going to sleep together on a big mattress..." either at the foot of your bed or in your three-year-old's own room. She will probably feel that although she has lost a bit of mommy, she has gained more of daddy with no overall net loss. You may also try a futon or a child's sleeping bag at the foot of your bed. It might be wise to begin these alternative sleeping arrangements before your new baby comes.

Q. I have heard that breastfed babies wake up more frequently. Is this true?

Yes. Studies comparing breast- and bottle-fed babies have shown that breastfed babies do, indeed, wake up more frequently. I believe there are two reasons for this. Breast milk, being digested more quickly, does not stay in the stomach as long as formula, so the breastfed infant may not have a feeling of fullness as long. Another reason that breastfed babies wake more often at night may be the conditioned responsiveness of the mother. A breastfeeding mother, perhaps owing to the biological effects of the hormone prolactin, is more likely to give an unrestrained nurturant response to her baby's cry. It is often more difficult for her to let her baby "cry it out" than it is for a bottle-feeding mother, because a breastfeeding mother has been conditioned to respond. Some sleep researchers call this "conditioned night waking."

The more a baby learns to anticipate being fed as soon as he awakens, perhaps the more he will continue to awaken. As a matter of fact, babies enjoy nursing at night, especially if mother has a busy lifestyle during the day. Can you blame them?

GLOSSARY

Attachment-promoting behaviors those behaviors of the infant that draw the caregiver to the newborn like a magnet; the most noteworthy is the infant's cry.

Baby-wearing carrying baby in a sling adjusted to fit the contours of parent's and baby's bodies, and according to the lifestyles of the parents and temperament of the baby.

Burnout emotional state of exhaustion when demands of a profession such as parenting exceed the available energy, resulting in the inability to continue functioning.

Colic the sounds and body language of a healthy baby who exhibits periodic bouts of screaming, drawing his legs up into a tense, gas-filled abdomen, clenching his fists, grimacing painfully, but seems completely healthy between outbursts.

Gastrointestinal reflux a condition in which some of the food in the baby's stomach is pushed back into the esophagus, causing a sensation similar to heartburn; one medical cause of colic.

High-need baby the fussy baby, one who is supersensitive, intense, demanding, hyperactive, restless, and craves physical contact and incessant holding.

Lactase an enzyme in breast milk that aids in digestion of lactose, or milk sugar.

Nature vs. nurture a phrase indicating the controversy among psychologists as to whether a child's temperament is due more to heredity or to environment.

Need level concept the theory that, from birth, every baby possesses a certain level of needs that must be fulfilled for the baby to reach his maximum potential. The need level concept leads to the important point that a baby fusses mainly because of his own temperament, not because of his parents' abilities.

Prolactin a hormone stimulated in the mother by breast-feeding; it appears to have a tranquilizing effect and to stimulate a higher level of maternal sensitivity.

REM sleep light sleep characterized by rapid eye movements. REM sleep constitutes 20% to 25% of adults' total sleep but up to 80% of infants'.

Rooming-in having mother and newborn share a room in the hospital, rather than keeping baby in the nursery.

Sharing sleep having a baby sleep with his parents; it is comforting to the baby and helps synchronize parents' and baby's sleep cycles.

Stimulus barrier the ability to selectively block out disturbing stimuli and receive pleasant stimuli; high-need babies tend to have a permeable stimulus barrier and are unable to block out disturbances.

INDEX

DR. BALTER'S STEPPING STONE STORIES

Dr. Lawrence Balter,
Illustrations by Roz Schanzer

Each of the storybooks in this series deals with a particular concern a young child might have about growing up. Each book features the same cast of characters—the kids who live in the fictional town of Crescent Canyon, a group to whom any youngster can relate. The stories are thoroughly entertaining while they help kids to understand their own feelings and the feelings of others. Engaging full-color illustrations fill every page! (Ages 3–7) Each book: Hardcover, $5.95, Can. $7.95, 40 pp., 8" x 8"

A Funeral for Whiskers:
Understanding Death ISBN: 6153-5

A.J.'s Mom Gets a New Job:
Adjusting to a Separation ISBN: 6151-9

Alfred Goes to the Hospital: Understanding
a Medical Emergency ISBN: 6150-0

Linda Saves the Day:
Understanding Fear ISBN: 6117-9

Sue Lee's New Neighborhood:
Adjusting to a New Home ISBN: 6116-0

Sue Lee Starts School:
Adjusting to School ISBN: 6152-7

The Wedding: Adjusting to a
Parent's Remarriage ISBN: 6118-7

What's the Matter With A.J.?:
Understanding Jealousy ISBN: 6119-5

ISBN PREFIX: 0-8120

Books may be purchased at your bookstore, or by mail from Barron's. Enclose check or money order for total amount plus sales tax where applicable and 10% for postage and handling (minimum charge $1.75, Canada $2.00). Prices are subject to change without notice.

Barron's Educational Series, Inc.
250 Wireless Boulevard
Hauppauge, NY 11788
Call toll-free: 1-800-645-3476
In NY: 1-800-257-5729

IN CANADA:
Georgetown Book Warehouse
34 Armstrong Avenue
Georgetown, Ontario L7G 4R9
Call toll-free: 1-800-247-7160